I0214282

Quaker Leaders Who Transformed the World

By David W. Kingrey D.Min.

Foreword by Derek Brown Ph.D.

Barclay College
PUBLISHERS

Barclay College Publishers

Quaker Leaders Who Transformed the World
Copyright © 2022 by David Kingrey, D.Min.

Requests for information should be addressed to:
Barclay College Publishers, 607 N. Kingman St, Haviland, KS 67059

Library of Congress Control Number: 2022945405
Hardcover ISBN: 978-1-7354646-3-3

All rights reserved. Published by Barclay College Publishers. No part of this book may be reproduced or transmitted in any form or by any means, electronic or mechanical, including photocopying, recording, or by an information storage and retrieval system—other than for "fair use" as brief quotations embodied in articles and reviews—without written permission from the publisher.

First Printing September 2022
Printed in the United States of America

Quaker Leaders Who Transformed the World
is written to the Glory of Our Divine Transformational Leader,
Jesus Christ
and
Dedicated to
Carol, Scott, David, and their families

TABLE OF CONTENTS

FOREWORD

I first met Dr. Dave Kingrey when I was an undergraduate student at Barclay College and enrolled in his Teachings of Friends (a survey of Quakerism) course. Not only had I never met him before, but I had little knowledge about Quakerism. However, I soon became acquainted with both. It was because of that class that I embarked on a journey that led to me becoming a convinced Friend, completing a Ph.D. with a dissertation on American Friends ecclesiology, teaching at a Friends Bible college, writing a book on Christ-centered Quaker pastoral theology, and now serving as Vice President for Academic Services at Barclay College. What connects those events (besides the obvious 'Quaker-ness') is that, from that first semester, Dave has been a positive presence in my life nearly every step of the way.

Here is where words fail me, for nowhere is my weakness as a wordsmith more apparent than my clumsy attempts to explain Dave's impact on my life since I first met him. I can say that he has been a professor, colleague, mentor, and friend. However, while these words convey the truth, they lack what Emily Dickinson called "phosphorescence." For as long as I have known him, he has been a model of Christlike charity, unceasing encouragement, boundless patience, and genuine caring for my family and me. His ministry experience has been a source of wisdom for my students and me, and his encyclopedic knowledge of Quakerism is matched only by his passion for seeing others know Christ. Thus, despite my authorial shortcomings, I am honored to write this foreword.

As a convinced Friend, I remember quickly realizing the simplicity of the Quaker message (for example, distinctively taking the commands of Christ and Scripture seriously in one's own life and interactions) was accompanied by a complex history of faithfulness and discernment incarnated in countless settings and situations. Without a guide, the breadth and depth of Quaker history make exploration daunting to the outsider. I was blessed to have Dave as my guide during my undergraduate years at college, where he patiently guided me and others through the triumphs, trials, conversions, controversies, history, theology, and the impact that Quakerism has had on the world.

But what of those without the benefit of such a guide? What of those seekers who lack a Friends church, meeting, or community of faith to disciple and teach about the Quaker expression of Christianity? Here, one sees the value of this resource and the wisdom in Dave's approach. Because while there are numerous Quaker histories available (including some that are as approachable in their tone and style as they are informative), Dr. Kingrey, through this book, has highlighted an essential truth: that a Friend should not have their fidelity to Christ measured by their words, but by their life. Thus, by letting these Quakers' 'lives speak,' Dave is helping make real what has, for many, become a historical footnote or marketing mascot.

The benefit of any expertly curated list is the thoughtfulness of the choices. I appreciate Dave's choices for this book, which reflect a deliberate intention to feature not only well-known historical Friends but also some contemporary Quakers from various contexts. Each biographical summary is clear and concise, with a length that allows the reader to study an individual in a single sitting. The content is also approachable, for Dave has wisely resisted the temptation to bog down the pages with footnotes containing rabbit trails and evidentiary asides, allowing for a smoother, uninterrupted reading experience. The bibliography should also be helpful to students or readers looking to do further research. The overall result is a text that is efficient, approachable, and avoids getting bogged down in extraneous details.

For those new to the Friends Church, this book provides an efficient and effective people's history of a Christian movement that God has used to change the world. For Friends more familiar with their history and tradition, it is a necessary reminder that our historical impact was never in our numerical size but in our passionate perseverance in following God's will. Furthermore, while it is easy to nostalgically view Quakerism's impact on this world as a historical relic, the timeline of this book leads the reader to realize that God may not be finished with Christian Quakerism yet (I do not think He is), but that He can and will use the movement (i.e., faithful individuals) to change the world in Jesus' name. I am grateful to Dr. Kingrey for this reminder and encouragement.

Derek Brown, Ph.D.
Haviland, KS

PREFACE

Quakers (Friends) have been well known as leaders since their origin in the mid-sixteen hundreds. By the grace of God, these leaders have transformed lives, indeed the world, throughout their history. During the years that I taught courses on Friends History and Beliefs at Barclay College, I became more aware of the transformational leadership of the Quakers. Their transformative power has come from their faithfulness to Jesus' teaching in John 15:14, "You are my friends if you do what I command you." Friends received their name from this passage of Scripture. *Quaker Leaders Who Transformed the World* gives a brief narrative of major Friends leaders in each century from the beginning of the Quaker movement to the present. These life sketches are not intended to be full biographies, but profiles of Quaker leaders, etched in their history-making roles of transforming lives, society, and the world. Hopefully, the reader will be inspired to research more deeply their lives and ministries that changed the world.

David W. Kingrey
Barclay College
2022

GEORGE FOX
1624-1691

"... When all my hopes ... in all men were gone, so that I had nothing outwardly to help me, nor could I tell what to do, then, Oh then, I heard a voice which said, 'There is one even Christ Jesus that can speak to thy condition,' and when I heard it my heart did leap for joy."
-George Fox

George Fox was born at Fenny Drayton in Leicester-shire, England. When he was young, Fox was an apprentice cobbler. He was raised in a Puritan church and attended worship services regularly with his devout parents, until age nineteen when he experienced disappointment, confusion, and spiritual unrest. He was confused by the inconsistency of professing Christians, whose lives did not reflect Christian values. So much of the religion around him seemed like empty formality. He traveled the countryside seeking a deeper religion. He talked with priests and other religious leaders but could find no spiritual satisfaction. Finally, in 1647 this seeker's life was transformed, and he became a finder. He found that only Christ could speak to his condition. Fox felt the immediate presence of Christ Jesus, and he was assured that Christ could be experienced directly, without a mediator. He knew that Christ had come to teach His people Himself.

George Fox had four compelling insights, which he called "openings," and these became foundational to Friends theology:

1. A Christian is one whose inner life is changed by Christ.
2. Every Christian is a minister and has a ministry to share.
3. The church is the fellowship of Christians, not a building.
4. Everyone can experience Christ directly.

George Fox knew the written Scriptures well. In fact it was said by some, that if all the Bibles in the world were burned, Fox could rewrite the Scriptures. He depended on the outward words of Scripture and the inward Word, Christ Jesus.

George Fox maintained a strong peace testimony. He was promised freedom from imprisonment if he would take up arms for the Commonwealth army and fight against the

King, but he refused, explaining that he lived in the virtue of the life and power that took away the occasion of war. He was opposed, not only to war, but also to the inward desires of anger, greed, and power that led to violence. He was committed to turn people from "darkness" to "light."

In 1652, George Fox climbed Pendle Hill, where he had a vision of "a great people to be gathered." He realized that there were thousands of religious seekers, who could be gathered into vital fellowship, and who could radically transform the church and the world. A short time later Fox preached for about three hours to a thousand seekers on Firbank Fell. These women and men went forth as ministers and missionaries, preaching the truth of Jesus Christ. About sixty of them were known as the Valiant Sixty. One of the Valiant Sixty was Margaret Fell, who was married to Judge Thomas Fell, and they lived at Swarthmoor Hall.

Eleven years after Thomas Fell's death, George Fox married Margaret Fell, and they ministered together until George's death in 1691. Their center of ministry was Swarthmoor Hall, where Friends gathered for worship, supported one another in fellowship, and provided care for Quakers suffering from persecution.

Fox traveled widely in the ministry, throughout England, on the continent of Europe, in Jamaica, Barbados, and in the American colonies, and because his beliefs countered those of the established church, he was arrested and imprisoned. Fox was jailed for a total of about six years during eight imprisonments, but his invincible spirit was not weakened.

George Fox, a man of vision, trustworthiness, and integrity, and whose life was centered in Christ Jesus, radically transformed religious beliefs and made possible the Friends Church as an enduring witness through the centuries.

Margaret Fell Fox
1614-1702

"Now, Friends, deal plainly with yourselves and let the Eternal Light search you . . . for this will deal plainly with you."
-Margaret Fell Fox

Margaret Fell is known as the "Mother of Quakerism." She was the most influential woman in the early days of the Friends movement. She was born at Marsh Grange, near Dalton-in-Furness, Lancashire, England. In 1632, she married Thomas Fell, who was a barrister. Later he became a judge and served in Parliament. She gave birth to seven daughters and one son. Six of the seven daughters became ministers. They lived in Swarthmoor Hall, owned by Thomas Fell, who was sympathetic to Quakers, but never became a Friend.

Margaret heard George Fox preach at Ulverston. He touched her heart profoundly. She stood up in her pew as he preached about the Spirit, who gave forth the Scriptures, and said that this Spirit could speak inwardly to them. She sat back down and cried bitterly to the Lord, expressing her sorrow, that she had known the Scriptures outwardly, but had not known them inwardly. She had a fresh understanding that God and Christ are not merely to be read about in a theology book, but can be known inwardly by all who open their hearts to the Lord. This was one of Fox's major "openings," that everyone can know Christ directly. Margaret's life was transformed by his powerful message, which spoke directly to her needs, and she became a Quaker. She made Swarthmoor Hall the headquarters for Friends, and it was a haven for Quakers who were suffering from persecutions.

Margaret was instrumental in the organization of Friends. She wrote many pamphlets and epistles to Friends workers in England and overseas and disbursed monetary funds to ministers and missionaries. She, herself, became a minister, and on one mission trip traveled, with two of her daughters, one thousand miles. She made ten trips from Northwest England to London to appeal to the King on behalf of suffering and imprisoned Quakers and to minister to Friends, who were experiencing difficulties and persecutions. She was a member of the Valiant Sixty, a group of ministers and missionaries, who went to strategic locations to share the gospel.

Margaret was an established member of the gentry, and, because of this, and Judge Fell's influence, she was successful in convincing prison officials to free Quaker prisoners, including George Fox. She had audiences with King Charles II, pleading the release of Fox. However, upon the death of Judge Fell in 1658, her power weakened. She was imprisoned two times for refusing to swear an oath of allegiance to the King, and for allowing Quaker worship to be held in her home. During her imprisonments, she wrote many pamphlets. One of these was *Women's Speaking Justified*, an argument based on Scripture for women ministers. She authored numerous books. She also wrote a declaration to the King, the Governors, and both Houses of Parliament, in which she explained the beliefs of Friends, including, the peace testimony.

Margaret married George Fox in 1669. They ministered together in the cause of Christ for the remainder of George's life. Yet they were often separated, particularly when George traveled to Barbados, Jamaica, the American colonies, Germany, and Holland.

Margaret Fell Fox was vital in the establishment of the Religious Society of Friends. She maintained her vision for the Quaker movement until she died in the arms of her youngest daughter, Rachel, whom she told in her dying breath that she was at peace. Her death left a deep hole in the Friends movement; however, because of her genius in organization, she prepared many others to carry forth the ministry.

ELIZABETH HOOTON
1600-1672

> *"The love of God beareth and suffereth, and envyeth no man."*
> *-Elizabeth Hooton*

Born Elizabeth Carrier in Nottinghamshire, England, she married Oliver Hooton and changed her name to Elizabeth Hooton. They moved to Skegby, where she became involved with the Baptists. When she met George Fox and listened to him preach, she held meetings in her home for other Baptists to hear Fox's messages. She soon joined the Quaker movement and remained a Friend for the duration of her life. She became the first woman Quaker preacher. She assumed her role as an itinerant minister and was one of the Valiant Sixty, a group of Quaker ministers, who often traveled in pairs, to share the gospel of Jesus Christ. Elizabeth endured severe persecution in her steadfast pursuit of the ministry. She was sent to prison in Derby for disapproving of a statement made by a priest. The next year she was again imprisoned, this time for preaching in a church in Rotherham.

After being released from prison, Hooton sailed to New England with Joan Brockstop. Although it was illegal for Quakers to enter Massachusetts, they went to Boston to visit Friends. For their presence in Boston, they were thrown into stocks, denied food, and beaten in three towns. They were taken to a forest, during the freezing temperatures of winter, and left there. They managed to survive by following wolf tracks through the snow to a settlement. Hooton left Massachusetts but returned later. She was again beaten, stripped of her clothing, and left in the wilderness.

After these persecutions, Hooton traveled back to England, where she met with the King and petitioned that he remedy the problem of Quaker persecutions in New England. The King gave Elizabeth authorization to buy land in Massachusetts, which she could use as a safe haven for Quakers in the colony. However, the safe haven was denied by the authorities in Massachusetts.

At age seventy-one, Elizabeth Hooton and George Fox journeyed to Jamaica. Fox became ill. She served as his nurse, but she was stricken with an illness and died the next day.

Elizabeth Hooton is remembered as a Quaker preacher, relentless to share the Truth of Christ in spite of great persecutions.

MARY DYER
1615-1660

"In obedience to the will of the Lord I came, and for His will I abide faithful to death."
-Mary Dyer

Mary Dyer was raised by Puritan parents in London. She married William Dyer in 1633. They settled in Boston, Massachusetts. There William befriended Roger Williams, and Mary became acquainted with Ann Hutchinson, who believed that God could speak directly to people, and they did not need an intermediary. Mary accepted her antinomian beliefs, which claimed that faith alone was sufficient for salvation. Sadly, Mary suffered a still-born baby. Governor Winthrop and the Puritans blamed Mary's still-born baby on her beliefs. Although the baby was buried privately, Winthrop had the body exhumed the next year. He described it as a monster, using terms such as an ape with horns, sharp pricks, scales, claws, two mouths, and many more ugly words. Winthrop published his description in several correspondences, including some in England, and declared that the deformed birth was evidence of Mary's mistaken antinomian beliefs.

Mary and William Dyer and Ann Hutchinson were banned from Massachusetts, and they moved to Rhode Island with the encouragement of Roger Williams. The Dyers returned to England in 1651, only to go again to America, William in 1653 and Mary in 1656. Mary had become a Quaker after hearing George Fox preach.

Mary began to preach and was arrested in New Haven, Connecticut. On her release, she traveled back to Massachusetts to visit two of her friends, William Robinson and Marmaduke Stevenson. Robinson had sailed on the ship, Woodhouse, the captain of which, was Robert Fowler. The ship was forced by storm to land for a short time on the south coast of England. There Robert Fowler said of the passengers, "They gathered sticks, and kindled a fire, and left it burning." This well-known saying is translated to mean that they gathered the inhabitants; they shared their message, as if kindling a fire, and left it burning among the people, who then shared the message with others. As they sailed on, the passengers on the Woodhouse heard an inward voice saying, "Cut through and steer your straightest course and mind nothing but me."

Dyer, Robinson, and Stevenson went to Massachusetts, where they were arrested and banned from the colony; however, the three of them returned and preached to a crowd. Robinson addressed the people first. He told them it was their day of visitation and to mind the light of Christ. A Puritan minister shouted to him that he would die with a lie in his mouth. Robinson answered, saying that he suffered for Christ and would die for Him. The rope was tightened, and he was hanged. Stevenson then stepped forward to the ladder and spoke to the crowd, explaining that the Quakers suffered, not as evil-doers, but for the sake of conscience, and they would be at peace with the Lord. He also was hanged. As Mary Dyer stepped up to the ladder, with her face covered and a halter around her neck, someone shouted that she was reprieved, and the execution was stopped. She was banished again from Massachusetts, but Mary, determined to do God's will, returned. Governor Endicott asked her if she was the same Mary Dyer who had been in Massachusetts before. She told him she was, and the death sentence was passed. A group of soldiers, beating drums, led her all the way to her place of execution. The sound of the drums prevented her from being heard by the crowd. The death walk was about a mile, during which she was strongly guarded, as if she were a violent criminal. Having climbed the ladder, again she was told that if she would return home she might save her life. She said she could not and spoke the words at the heading of this biographical profile. Someone told her that she should have said she would be in paradise, to which she answered that she had been in paradise several days. The rope was tightened around her neck, and she breathed her last breath.

Statues of Mary Dyer are on the Earlham College campus, for which Elton Trueblood was partially responsible, at the Friends Center in Philadelphia, and diagonally across from Boston Common, near the place where she was hanged. They stand as a reminder that Mary Dyer, a transforming Quaker leader, was willing to give her life in obedience to God.

MARY FISHER
1623-1698

When Mary Fisher was asked what she thought of Mohammed, she answered, "I confess I know him not. But the true prophet, the Son of God, who is the Light of the world and enlighteneth every man coming into the world, Him I know."
-Mary Fisher

Mary Fisher's life as a Quaker began when she heard George Fox preach in Yorkshire, England. She was convinced by Fox's message that Christ Jesus is the true Inward Teacher and Guide. She became a member of the Valiant Sixty, a group of ministers, who often traveled in pairs to share the good news of Christ. On her first missionary journey, she was not welcome. She was arrested and thrown into prison in York Castle for speaking to a priest. There she developed a friendship with Elizabeth Hooton and Thomas Aldam. When released from prison, Mary set out with Elizabeth Williams for Cambridge, where they addressed a group of men students, who jeered and mocked these women ministers. Soon others mocked them, and they were arrested by the mayor and whipped in public until blood ran from their bodies. Both women knelt in prayer, asking God to forgive the mayor, yet they were taken to the marketplace, where they were commanded to remove their clothes. They refused, so the guard stripped them naked to the waist, forced their arms into the whipping post, and brutally whipped them until they were terribly bruised and cut. Mary left Cambridge and returned to her home in Yorkshire, where she was imprisoned in York Castle for speaking to a priest.

Soon after she was released from prison, she and Ann Austin crossed the Atlantic, landing first at Barbados, where they were warmly greeted, and their ministry was accepted. After their time on the Caribbean island, they set sail for New England. Richard Bellingham, Deputy Governor of Boston, considered Quakers blasphemers, trouble makers, and disrespectful of authority. He thought they were worthy only to be burned and hanged publically. He tried to stamp out the Quakers. When Fisher and Austin came ashore, they were imprisoned in a dark cell. They were denied food, bedding, and Bibles. Their isolation was to prevent them from corrupting the citizens. After five weeks of these dehumanizing conditions, Fisher and Austin were shipped back to Barbados, where they ministered freely.

Mary Fisher returned to England, and in 1657, she with a small group of Friends, set out on a voyage to lands further east. John Perrot was their leader, and he desired to see the Pope. Mary Fisher was being led by God to talk with the Sultan of Turkey. When the ship stopped at Smyrna, the British consul, thinking her trip to Turkey was too dangerous, put her on a ship to return to England. Determined to go to Turkey, Fisher persuaded the captain of the ship to permit her to go ashore at the next port. There she set out on foot, alone, to walk six hundred miles through Greece, Macedonia, and the mountains of Thrace to Andrianople, where the Sultan was encamped with his soldiers. The journey was remarkable, considering that she had limited resources. She could speak only English, and some of the territory was under control of the powerful Turks. However, nothing could stop Mary Fisher from following God's calling. When she arrived at the encampment, the Sultan greeted her warmly. She told him she had a message from God, and he considered her an ambassador from the highest power. He was arrayed with a gold cloth. Around him were court officials with colorful costumes. Mary was wearing only her simple Quaker dress, which must have been well worn after six hundred miles of travel. She gave a simple message, which the Sultan heard through the aid of interpreters. At the end of her message, Mary asked him if he understood her. He answered that he did and that every word was the truth. When Mary was about to leave, she was offered an armed escort through dangerous territory, but she refused, believing that God would provide her safety. Before leaving, Mary was asked what she thought of Mohammed. The quotation at the top of this biographical profile was her answer. Then she set out alone to Constantinople.

We remember Mary Fisher as a Quaker leader, who had an indomitable spirit, a deep commitment to fulfill God's will, a passion to preach the love of Christ, and a willingness to endure the most severe punishment for the sake of Christian truth.

JAMES PARNELL
1636-1656

> *"I charge you all in the name of the God of Truth, be faithful, valiant, and bold for the Truth received: And as you have received it, so walk in it."*
> *-James Parnell*

James Parnell was a frail child and small in stature. He was plagued with childhood illnesses; nevertheless, he developed a questioning mind. His questions to his parents seemed endless. Parnell approached ministers for answers. Dissatisfied with their responses, he accused some of them for not practicing what they preached. They were critical of him, and his parents became impatient with him. Parnell finally found listening ears from the seekers, persons seeking deeper religious truths. Parnell walked many miles to talk and worship with the seekers, some of whom told him that he might find answers to his questions from George Fox. But Fox was one hundred fifty miles away in prison at Carlisle. Parnell, age sixteen, determined to meet Fox, walked the entire distance. It was a lonely walk through the moors. Occasionally he was given hospitality and meals in the homes of the seekers, who would also wash his clothes. Finally, with shoes that were worn out and clothes that were torn, young James arrived at Carlisle. At the prison he asked to talk with George Fox. The prison officials would not let him see Fox, because, they said, Fox's life would be endangered by violent criminals and murderers as he walked to talk with James. After persistence, Parnell, while being kicked, was given permission to enter the dungeon. He heard prisoners mocking Fox and yelling his name. Feeling lonely, he felt Fox's hand on his shoulder, and his loneliness suddenly dissipated. Fox answered his questions and spoke to him about Christ Jesus. Soon the jail keeper forced James out of the prison.

From that time forward little James had no home, except the homes of the seekers. He was told about the persecutions of Elizabeth Williams and Mary Fisher in Cambridge, where Parnell then traveled to preach. He was imprisoned and met Richard Hubberthorne from Yealand. After his release from prison, he was treated brutally, being knocked down and struck with a staff, but this brutality did not stop young James. He went to Colchester, where he stayed with Thomas and Ann Shortland, who were among his first converts. Attending a worship service in Colchester, he replied to the preacher, and in so doing, was arrested with the charge of inciting a riot. He was locked up in Colchester Castle to await trial. He was not allowed to see anyone. In handcuffs, and chained with six men, he walked twenty-two miles to stand trial. The jury could find no reason to convict James, but the judge took the law into his own hands, fined Parnell for contempt of court, and locked him up in Colchester Castle until he could pay the fine. This amounted to a life sentence. He was confined to a dark hole in the prison wall, with a floor of cold stones, where the rain would leak in and keep him wet. The hole was called the "oven," because it was like an oven, with no way to let in fresh air. The only access to the hole was a ladder, but it did not reach to the opening above. The only way for Parnell to receive his meals was to climb the ladder, then pull himself up on a rope that extended to the opening. It was a perilous act, because he had to hold the food in one hand and hold the rope in the other. One day when obtaining his meal, his hand slipped on the rope, and he fell to the stone floor below. He was knocked unconscious. When he regained consciousness, he was too weak to climb the rope again. Thomas Shortland begged the prison officials to allow him to take Parnell's place in prison, but they denied the request.

One night his prison cell door was accidentally left open, and Parnell limped out. The jail keeper found him and locked the door to his cell, so he could not get back in. This occurred during winter, and Parnell was forced to spend the night in the cold. The Shortlands stayed close to James, during the brief remainder of his life, and Parnell died at the age of twenty in their loving presence.

James Parnell, among the first of the Quaker martyrs, knew Christ personally, and preached the truth of Christ, who could speak to his condition, as Christ spoke to George Fox's condition. He bore testimony to God as a teenager, and thus showed that Quaker youths also could be transformational leaders.

WILLIAM PENN
1644-1718

"Christ's cross is Christ's way to Christ's crown."
-William Penn

William Penn grew up in a well-to-do family. His father, Sir William Penn, was an Admiral in the British navy. When young William was twelve years of age, Admiral Penn invited Thomas Loe, a Quaker, to his home to learn more about the Quakers. Loe became a mentor to young William Penn. For the next four years, William studied diligently and entered Oxford University at the age of sixteen. Penn made good grades, but he and a group of other students, disagreed with some of the University's policies. The University expelled Penn, and he went to study in France. There he met Moses Amyraut, whose teachings were similar to those of the Quakers. Two years later, while in Ireland on legal matters for the family, Penn met with the Quakers, and for the second time encountered Thomas Loe. Penn heard Loe speak. He was deeply moved and decided to take his place with the suffering Quakers. Then suddenly soldiers rushed in and took many of the worshipping Quakers to jail. Penn voluntarily went with them. Immediately he appealed to an influential person he knew, and everyone was released.

Penn became an active writer and preacher. A book that he wrote on the Trinity angered the ecclesiastical powers, and they demanded that he retract statements in the book. Refusing to do so, Penn was imprisoned in the Tower of London. During the time of his imprisonment, he wrote the book, *No Cross, No Crown*, the source of the quotation above.

Another historical incident in Penn's life was his trial with William Meade, known as the Penn-Meade trial. Less than two years after Penn's release from the Tower of London, he and other Quakers were assembled on Gracechurch Street in London. Officials had locked the doors of the meetinghouse, so Penn preached outside on the street. Penn and another Friend, William Meade, were arrested and quickly brought to trial. They were charged with inciting a riot. Lord Mayor Starling was determined to force a jury of twelve men to bring a charge of guilty. However, the jury did not agree with the guilty charge. Several times the jury was called in, and each time Starling demanded that they charge Penn and Meade guilty. The jury was even refused food, drink, heat, and other necessities, until they would pronounce these Quakers guilty. The jury continued to declare the men innocent. As a result, the members of the jury were all heavily fined and sent to Newgate Prison. This trial went down in history as helping to ensure the right of jury to have freedom from the judge.

William Penn is well known for his work in America. Because Admiral Penn had made a sizeable monetary loan to King Charles II, the King was approached for a favor in return. The result was a grant of land in America, which became known as Pennsylvania, meaning "Penn's Woods." It was named after Admiral Penn. William Penn had a plan he called the "Holy Experiment" that transformed the United States government. He drew up a constitution, some of the articles of which, became the basis for the United States Constitution. Citizens were given liberty to worship according to their own beliefs, freedom of speech, trials by jury, voting rights, and elections each year. All the laws were humane. The "Holy Experiment" had no forts and no soldiers. Prisons were transformed into schools. Penn paid the Native Americans for their land. He made a peace treaty with the Native Americans at Shackamaxon. It is estimated that Penn made treaties with twenty tribal leaders. William Penn also created a plan for the organization of nations, which was a forerunner of the United Nations.

Penn returned to England and met with his close friend, King James II. His influence on James led to greater toleration in England, the culmination of which was the Act of Toleration under William and Mary. It gave freedom to Quakers and all other religious groups in England. On both sides of the Atlantic, Penn was influential in giving freedom of religious expression.

William Penn's influence lives on, and his principles of liberty and peace continue to be an answer for our world. Penn suffered, bearing a cross, so that the crown of freedom, justice, and peace would prevail.

Robert Barclay
1648-1690

> *"There is an evangelical and saving light and grace in everyone, and the love and mercy of God toward mankind were universal, both in the death of his beloved Son, the Lord Jesus Christ, and in the manifestation of the light in the heart."*
> *-Robert Barclay*

Robert Barclay was born in Gordonstown, on the north coast of Scotland. His father was Colonel David Barclay, who sat in two of Oliver Cromwell's Parliaments. Robert was related to the House of Stuart through his mother, Catherine, of the Gordon family. The Barclays owned a great estate, Ury.

Robert was raised a strict Calvinist but studied in Scots Theological College, a Roman Catholic school in Paris. His uncle, another Robert Barclay, for whom he was named, was a teacher there. But he returned home at his dying mother's request. Two years later he came under the influence of the Quaker, John Swinton, when visiting his father in prison at Edinburgh Castle. Swinton was a cell mate of Colonel Barclay. The exposure to Swinton and his Quaker beliefs was crucial to Robert's own faith. He was convinced that he should become a Quaker in 1666 when worshipping with Friends and experiencing a "secret power" causing him to feel the evil in him weakening and the good raised up.

Robert Barclay married Christian Molleson in 1670. Their wedding was conducted in the traditional Quaker manner. Robert and Christian merely stood together in the presence of other Friends gathered for worship and declared their vows to each other. It was considered scandalous, because a clergyman was not present. Robert and Christian became the ancestors of the Barclays in the banking firm and the Gurneys of Earlham.

In his Quaker ministry, Robert experienced severe imprisonment in Aberdeen. He traveled with George Fox, William Penn, and George Keith to Holland and Germany, where they promoted the beliefs of Friends. Barclay was also appointed Governor of East Jersey (now a part of New Jersey).

Robert had a brilliant mind and wrote an apology, which was an intellectual formulation and defense of the Quaker faith. The full title of his work is *An Apology for the True Christian Divinity Being an Explanation and Vindication of the Principles and Doctrines of the People Called Quakers*. The *Apology* was published first in Latin in 1676, when he was only twenty-seven years old, and then in English in 1678. The *Apology* set forth the beliefs of Friends in a systematic way in fifteen propositions. In it he contended that the true knowledge of God is the height of all happiness. He affirmed the belief that God can speak to everyone through inward and unmediated revelation. He referred to John 1:9, which claims that the saving light of Christ enlightens everyone. Therefore, every person has the possibility of salvation. Barclay could not accept the notion that people, who lived before the Christ of history, or who, by misfortune, never heard of Jesus, are condemned. Christ has witnessed inwardly to everyone, yet each person must respond positively to Christ's inward leading, and not resist it. Barclay's emphasis on the inward light of Christ in no way diminished the importance of the Scriptures. Evidence is his quoting numerous passages from the Bible in each proposition. Throughout the *Apology*, Barclay emphasized the inward experience of the Christian faith, particularly in worship, baptism, and communion. In his fifteenth proposition, he appealed to Christians to have a living reverence for God and to be leavened with the evangelical spirit.

Only weeks before the death of George Fox, Robert died at the early age of forty-two, when on a visit to Scotland. Christian continued much of Robert's work after his death. The addition of Robert Barclay to the Quaker movement, during the years of fierce persecution, was central to the survival of Quakerism. Indeed, he made a permanent contribution to Quaker theology, and the *Apology* remains a foremost theology book for Friends today.

DR. JOHN FOTHERGILL
1712-1780

"I loved to be at home with my friends and to labor with my hands in the creation."
-Dr. John Fothergill

Dr. John Fothergill, named for his grandfather, was born into a Quaker family in York, England. John and his younger brother, Samuel, attended an elementary school in Sedbergh. He was gifted and had an inclination toward medicine. At the age of sixteen he was apprenticed with Benjamin Bartlett, a Quaker apothecary. He attended the University of Edinburgh, which did not require students to be members of the Church of England. John was prepared, he had a brilliant mind, insightful thought, the discipline of hard work, and the gift of making clear diagnosis. Important, also, to his being a good physician were his kind disposition and caring spirit. He cared for others, whether they were wealthy or poor. Often, without charge, he gave medical treatment to patients with meager or no income. As the quotation above indicates, he enjoyed giving hospitality to his friends in Carr End, a stone farmhouse, which he built. It was his lifetime home. He also appreciated God's natural creation, which the rural setting provided.

Fothergill traveled extensively. He made trips to America, where he sometimes walked through wilderness to reach people to whom he could minister, as did George Fox, whose *Journal* greatly influenced him. Fothergill had conversations with John Woolman and developed a personal relationship with Benjamin Franklin, who became his patient. Franklin went to England where he, John Fothergill, and David Barclay, grandson of Robert Barclay, drew up a document to bring a conciliatory relationship between England and America to prevent the Revolutionary War. They were terribly grieved when their efforts failed. Like William Penn, Fothergill committed to the Quaker peace testimony, also envisioned a league for the establishment of world peace. The United Nations is the fulfillment of his dream.

John Fothergill gave strong leadership to the Society of Friends. He was an advocate of quality Quaker education. When learning that the buildings of the Ackworth branch of a London hospital were for sale, he pioneered the way for Quakers to purchase them and use them for a school. They became known as Ackworth School. It was a model for other schools in England and America. In Philadelphia, Friends looked to Ackworth for the development of the school now known as Westtown School. Fothergill worked tirelessly for Ackworth School. He assisted in the organization of the school, raised financial support for it, and recruited administrators and teachers. Ackworth revolutionized Quaker education. Ackworth Friends Meeting in Iowa Yearly Meeting is named for the school. The Ackworth Friends meetinghouse was built only a few miles from the home place of Elton Trueblood, whose life and ministry revolved around education. Trueblood has been a guest speaker there.

Other accomplishments of Dr. John Fothergill included a more effective treatment of scarlet fever during an epidemic in London. He wrote up an account for diphtheria, in the course of an outbreak. He composed medical descriptions of tuberculosis, hydrophobia, and epilepsy. He was an advocate for the newly-developed vaccine against small pox. Catherine the Great of Russia sent her ambassador in London to consult with Dr. Fothergill. He recommended that she be vaccinated, and a Quaker doctor went to Russia and inoculated her. During an influenza epidemic, he treated more than sixty patients a day.

Beyond the worlds of medicine and education, Fothergill studied botany and cultivated many plants. He was opposed to slavery and befriended Anthony Benezet, a Philadelphia abolitionist. His work was broad and varied, and he ministered effectively to numerous people. Dr. John Fothergill lived in the spirit of Christ, the Divine Physician, in his practice of medicine and in his lifestyle of love for God's people, and thereby was a Quaker leader, who transformed the world.

John Woolman
1720-1772

> *"To turn all the treasures we possess into the channel of universal love becomes the business of our lives . . . To labor for the perfect redemption of this spirit of oppression is the great business of the whole family of Jesus Christ in our world . . . There was a care on my mind so to pass my time that nothing might hinder me from the most steady attention to the voice of the true Shepherd."*
> *-John Woolman*

There were more than ten million reported captives, who were forced to go by ship to the Americas and the islands of the Caribbean. Approximately one in eight died during the voyage. Into this despicably evil world of slavery walked John Woolman.

Woolman was born in West Jersey, now a portion of New Jersey. From childhood he was spiritually sensitive, simple in lifestyle, obedient, and humble. At age twenty he moved from the family farm to Mount Holly, where he worked at a bakery, and regularly attended a Friends Meeting. John became very concerned about people around him, who were living worldly lives, and sometimes he felt compelled to talk with them about their lifestyles. Woolman's conscience toward the needs of others came to a head when he was asked to write a bill of sale for a person to become a slave. Although he felt uneasy about writing an instrument of slavery, in weakness, he did so. Afterward, he was mentally convicted, and when he was asked to write a bill of sale in the future, he refused.

Woolman's convictions about the evil of slavery grew, and he traveled long distances to labor for the freedom of slaves. He journeyed to Maryland, North Carolina, Connecticut, Massachusetts, and Rhode Island. Woolman's influence was significant, and his style was powerful, sometimes silently powerful. He often witnessed by his actions. For example, when staying with slave owners, he refused free hospitality given by the slaves. Instead, he left money with the slave owners to give to the slaves in payment for the services they gave him. In 1758 he was hosted by Thomas Woodward. Woolman noticed servants and learned that they were slaves, yet he was silent about his belief against slavery. Later that night, getting out of bed, he wrote a note to the Woodwards, explaining the reason he could not accept their hospitality. He went to the slaves' quarters, paid them for their services, and walked out into the dark. Woolman's silent testimony pierced the heart of Thomas Woodward, and he set free all of his slaves. Further evidence of Woolman's convictions against slavery were his refusal to eat sugar processed by slaves, to drink from silver cups made by slaves, and to wear dyed clothing, because the dyes were made by slaves.

Woolman's testimony against slavery climaxed in the 1758 gathering of Philadelphia Yearly Meeting. This was the great watershed for Quakers on the slavery issue. The preliminary debates on slavery were intense and controversial. Woolman was intent to have them resolved. After many proposals had been offered, during which Woolman was silent, finally with tears in his eyes, he rose and spoke.

In his speech he told the assembly that God is just, and Friends should not neglect their just duty toward the deliverance of slaves. Woolman's message had such a powerful effect on the Yearly Meeting members that their decision, without a single dissent, was to remove slavery from the Yearly Meeting. Eventually other Yearly Meetings followed Philadelphia Yearly Meeting's decision, and slavery was removed from the Religious Society of Friends. In great measure, through Woolman's transforming leadership, Quakerism in America was free from the taint of slavery long before Abraham Lincoln was born. By 1784 all North American Yearly Meetings officially prohibited slavery among their members. Quakers were the first religious group to denounce slavery publicly and the first to require members to free slaves. Furthermore, Quakers were asked to reimburse slaves for their time in bondage.

Woolman also maintained strong convictions about peace. He was opposed to violence. For example, prior to the Revolutionary War, the government officials ordered him to make accommodations in his home for soldiers. The order troubled Woolman. He decided that if soldiers were sent to him, he would not deny them hospitality, but he would refuse financial compensation to keep them.

Woolman had a heart for Native Americans. He sometimes traveled through hostile territory, having only one companion with him. He accepted the hospitality of Native Americans, and without the aid of interpreters, he prayed for them. Showing his cultural sensitivity, when going on missionary journeys, often before sharing his message, he told the Native Americans that he came to learn from them.

Woolman was a person of simplicity. He realized that wealth often led to the desire for more wealth. He wrote, *A Plea for the Poor*, in which he set forth a case for persons caught in poverty.

In summary, Woolman was committed to following Christ faithfully and to listening with "the most steady attention to the voice of the true Shepherd." In so doing, he was a powerful Quaker leader, who transformed untold numbers of lives, indeed the world. After writing an essay on John Woolman, in a course on Quaker History and Beliefs at Barclay College, an African American student commented, "I never realized that the Quakers did so much for my people." What a tribute!

STEPHEN GRELLET
1773-1855

> *"I expect to pass through this world but once. Any good, therefore, that I can do, or any kindness that I can show to anyone, let me do it now. Let me not defer nor neglect it, for I shall not pass this way again."*
> *-Stephen Grellet*

Stephen Grellet was born into a wealthy family in France. When the French Revolution broke out, the family had to flee. Stephen was captured and sentenced to death, but he escaped to Amsterdam. From Holland he sailed to the West Indies and on to New York.

One day he was walking in a field when suddenly he heard a voice shouting, "Eternity! Eternity! Eternity!" This caused him to shake with fear. Following that transforming experience, he read William Penn's *No Cross, No Crown* twice, and Penn's words affected him profoundly. Later, Deborah Darby, a Quaker minister, had a great influence on Grellet. He soon joined the Friends movement and became a minister. In his ministry, he traveled throughout America, England, Ireland, and the continent of Europe. In his lifespan,

Grellet traveled nearly one hundred thousand miles. His primary message was that Jesus is the Son of God, the Lamb of God, and the Savior of sinners. During the Great Separation among Friends in 1827 and 1828, he was a leader of the Orthodox branch of Quakers, professing the divinity and salvation of Christ, the authority of the Bible, and advocating programmed worship.

Stephen Grellet is noted for his faithfulness to God's guidance. He felt God leading him to go into a woods and preach. He rode on his horse into the woods, where he saw a clearing. There was a worker's shanty. He dismounted his horse and prayed for guidance. He heard a voice telling him to give God's message there. He could see no one, yet with his heart and soul, he preached a full-length sermon. His message was about God's forgiving love. Following the sermon, he felt discouraged, confused, and foolish. This occurred in New Jersey. Sometime later he went to London where he had a surprising experience. He was crossing the London Bridge when a man tapped him on the shoulder who was excited to see him. Grellet did not recognize the man, who told Grellet that he heard him preach. He explained that he was working in some woods one day and returned to a shanty to retrieve a tool. He heard someone preaching, so he listened, peered through a crack in the wall of the shanty, and saw Grellet. He told Grellet that his message went through a crack in his heart also. Until that time he did not believe in God, but after hearing Grellet, he found a Bible and searched at length until he found Grellet's Scripture text on God's forgiving love. He then went to his godless friends, who laughed at him as he told them about Grellet's sermon on the forgiveness of God. However, he convinced his friends, and he explained to Grellet, that three of them became missionaries. As a result, he thought a thousand people had found the Lord.

As cultured and wise as Grellet was, he ministered among the monarchs of Europe. He interviewed the Pope, addressed bishops, nuns, and priests in the Roman Catholic Church, and spoke to Protestant clergy. Grellet preached to the poor and visited slaves. He had a spiritual concern for prisoners awaiting death in Newgate Prison. There the conditions were horrific with filth, misery, and stench. In the infirmary he saw sick prisoners and newborn babies lying on the cold floor. He felt he had to do something to improve the conditions, so he rushed to Elizabeth Fry and appealed to her to minister to the Newgate prisoners. She responded in a major way, as we can see in reading her biographical profile in this book.

Stephen Grellet, Quaker leader, is a great example of a person obedient to God. In his obedience he transformed the lives of people in many parts of the world.

ELIZABETH GURNEY FRY
1780-1845

> *". . . I believe that I never have awakened from sleep, in sickness or in health, by day or by night, without my first awakening thought being how best I might serve my Lord."*
> *-Elizabeth Gurney Fry*

Elizabeth Gurney Fry was the daughter of John and Catherine Gurney. John was a partner in the Norwich Bank in England. Catherine was the great-granddaughter of Robert Barclay. They had twelve children. One of her brothers was Joseph John Gurney. The family's place of residence was Earlham Hall. Betsy, as she was called in her younger years, had a happy childhood. She wore colorful clothes, quite a contrast to the Quaker plain dress. She was seen wearing purple boots, laced with scarlet, as she sat in Meeting for Worship. At age seventeen she was introduced to William Savery, a Philadelphia Quaker, who preached with power. Elizabeth was deeply moved by his sermon. The next morning Savery spoke to her and told her she had an important calling awaiting her. Soon afterward, when her father took her to London, she heard Savery preach again. When returning to Earlham Hall, she decided that the high life of London was not for her. Elizabeth gave up the frivolities of life, and began wearing the plain dress and using the plain language of "thee" and "thou" that characterized Quakers. Later she met Deborah Darby, the same Deborah Darby who influenced Stephen Grellet. Darby told her that she would be a light to the blind, the voice for those who could not speak, and feet for those who were lame.

In 1800 Elizabeth married Joseph Fry. At age thirty-one she was recorded as a minister. Later she met Stephen Grellet, who told her of the pressing needs in Newgate Prison. Immediately she began visiting the prisoners, against the advice of prison officials, who explained to her that her life would be endangered by violent prisoners. Nevertheless, Elizabeth was bound to bring reform amidst the atrocious prison conditions. She found mothers with children running wild and convinced the mothers of a need for a school. She enlisted one of the mothers to help teach. She also offered Bible studies for women prisoners.

Elizabeth's work took her into the medical ministry. She established a training school for nurses, and some of Florence Nightingale's nurses were trained in her school.

In other work, Fry convinced the British government

to provide libraries for its naval hospitals. The result was six hundred libraries with fifty-two thousand, four hundred volumes. Elizabeth was instrumental in the founding of Swarthmore College, the Friends Medical College of Pennsylvania, and the School of Design for Women (now Moore College of Art and Design) in Philadelphia. She visited the King of Prussia. Also of interest, is that her picture appears on the five pound British Note.

Elizabeth's life tells the importance of the Quaker fellowship and the influence of leaders to inspire future leaders. As William Savery, Deborah Darby, and Stephen Grellet faithfully ministered to Elizabeth, she steadfastly ministered to untold numbers of others. Elizabeth Fry beautifully exemplified the answer to the question of the righteous in Jesus' Parable of the Last Judgment in Matthew 25:39-40. The righteous asked when it was that they saw the Lord sick and in prison and visited him. The Lord answered, "Truly, I tell you, just as you did it to one of the least of these who are members of my family, you did it to me" (Matthew 25:40). Elizabeth visited the "least" of Christ's family, and therefore she visited Christ.

Joseph John Gurney
1788-1847

"The mercy of God in Christ Jesus is a subject I have long been accustomed to regard as superior to all others in point of interest and importance."
-Joseph John Gurney

Joseph John Gurney was a very influential Quaker leader. He was the son of John and Catherine Gurney and a younger brother of Elizabeth Gurney Fry. As a youth he did well in his education and went on to Oxford to study, even though he knew that he would not be granted a degree because he was not an Anglican. He continued his scholarship throughout his lifetime. He studied the Scriptures in their original languages. While he relied heavily upon the Bible, he also depended on guidance from the Holy Spirit. His primary purpose in life was to be a faithful follower of Jesus Christ.

Gurney was a banker. The Norwich Bank in England, of which he was head, became a branch of the chain of banks known as Barclay Banks. He used his home, Earlham Hall, to host the Anti-Slavery Society in Norwich and the annual meeting of the Bible Society. Gurney's scholarly pursuits and social action work led naturally to his writing ministry. His books reinforced the theology of Robert Barclay, of whom he was a descendant.

His prosperity in the banking business enabled him to travel and minister widely. His three-year trip to America was most successful. In Richmond, Indiana he had an audience of nearly six thousand listeners. A result of his success in Richmond was the naming of the School, Earlham College, after his place of residence, Earlham Hall. He journeyed also to the Guilford area of North Carolina and to Washington, where he addressed the joint Houses of Congress and was greeted by John Quincy Adams and Henry Clay. President Van Buren was present, and Gurney was successful in having an interview with him. He spent three years in America and the West Indies and accepted no salary during that time.

Joseph John Gurney was a major leader among the Evangelicals during the separations in 1845 and 1854. The Evangelicals were known as the Gurneyites. This branch of Quakers became the present-day Evangelical Friends Church International and Friends United Meeting. The Gurneyites emphasized the Divinity of Christ, progressive Christian education methods, programmed worship, and the authority of Scripture, accompanied by the indwelling of the Holy Spirit.

Joseph John Gurney was a deeply Christian man, with the highest form of integrity. As a Bible scholar, banker, writer, traveling minister, host, and anti-slavery activist, his death ended a great period in the Norwich area and on both sides of the Atlantic. The week between his death and memorial service, windows in homes were darkened, and shops were closed in memory of Joseph John Gurney. He steadfastly did what Jesus commanded, and as a result, he was a Quaker leader, who transformed innumerable lives.

Lucretia Coffin Mott
1793-1880

"I thought at that moment that I was willing to suffer, whatever the cause required."
-Lucretia Coffin Mott

Lucretia Coffin Mott was the second of seven children of Thomas and Anna Coffin, and grew up on Nantucket Island. Thomas was a sea captain, and Anna managed a shop. Lucretia was a lively girl and learned needlework from her mother. She attended Nine Partners Boarding School, now known as Oakwood School in New York. There she became an assistant teacher and was regarded as an apprentice without pay. James Mott also was an assistant teacher. Eventually Lucretia and James married. One of their children, Thomas, died, and his death was a shattering experience for both of them. From the agony, a deepened spiritual life arose in Lucretia. For the first time she spoke in Meeting for Worship, and this was the beginning of her public ministry. She studied the writings of William Penn and read George Fox's *Journal*, Robert Barclay's *Apology*, and John Woolman's *Journal*. She and James joined the anti-slavery cause and opened their home as a station on the Underground Railroad. During their ministry to slaves, they encountered a dramatic incident in which a fugitive slave, called "Henry Box Brown," had himself boxed and dispatched with a shipment from Richmond, Virginia to the anti-slavery office in Philadelphia, where the Motts were living. When the box was opened, Henry was alive and well, although stiff from having been boxed up for a lengthy period of time. He visited James and Lucretia in their home, and they sent him on his way to the next station on the Underground Railroad.

James and Lucretia had financial hardship. James was involved in the cotton business, but since cotton goods were produced in part by slaves, he gave up his lucrative work. Instead he began handling goods made from wool, a less profitable trade. In their anti-slavery work, James and Lucretia were involved in the great Philadelphia Anti-Slavery Convention, organized by William Lloyd Garrison and attended by the Quaker poet, John Greenleaf Whittier. It was an all-male gathering, but women were invited as spectators. However, during one of the sessions, Lucretia rose to her feet twice and spoke. Growing from this convention, the Anti-Slavery Society was founded, yet women were still not privileged to be members. Determined that women have a voice in the anti-slavery movement, Lucretia was instrumental in the founding of the Female Anti-Slavery Society. During this time, the anti-abolitionist sentiment grew, and after burning Pennsylvania Hall, a hostile anti-abolitionist mob marched to destroy the home of James and Lucretia. The quotation above by Lucretia occurred during this dangerous time and reflects her uttermost trust in God. The Motts were saved by one of their friends, who led the mob in the wrong direction.

A relationship formed between Lucretia and Elizabeth Cady Stanton. They and other women organized the historic Women's Rights Convention in Seneca Falls, New York. During the convention, resolutions were passed for women to be given equal opportunity with men to vote, to testify in court, to make contracts, to enter into professions, to be given property rights, and to have custody of children. In addition to her anti-slavery and women's rights ministry, Lucretia supported the peace and temperance movements.

An amusing story is told about Lucretia Mott, which highlights her honesty. She owned an apple orchard and became alarmed about the theft of apples from the orchard, not because she was worried about the loss of apples, but because she was concerned about the souls of the thieves. She settled the matter by placing a basket of apples outside her house, with a sign, "Thou shalt not steal." Below it she wrote, "Help Thyself."

Lucretia Mott, an activist for women's suffrage, abolition of slavery, temperance, and peace indelibly marked history. She was a woman of great courage and devotion to God.

She was a friend of the oppressed, and an African American male gave her a public farewell at her memorial service.

LEVI COFFIN
1798-1877

"Both my parents and grandparents were opposed to slavery, and none of either family ever owned slaves; and all were friends of the oppressed, so I claim that I inherited my anti-slavery principles."
-Levi Coffin

Levi Coffin was the son of Quakers Levi and Prudence Coffin, and grew up on a farm in Guilford County, North Carolina. His formal schooling was minimal, because his parents needed him to work on the farm. However, his six sisters educated him well, and he became a teacher and writer. He wrote his life story in *Reminiscences of Levi Coffin.*

At age seven, Levi was at the roadside where his father was chopping wood, and he witnessed slaves chained together in coffles. In subsequent years, he watched many of these chained slaves being forced by slave drivers with whips. He saw slaves being sold and separated from their families on auction blocks. He was deeply and negatively impressed. These experiences were central to Coffin's life commitment to anti-slavery work.

Coffin was instrumental in developing a Sabbath school in the New Garden area and taught slaves to read the Bible. He was a leader in the development of the Underground Railroad, which had many secret passageways for slaves to escape from the South to the North and to Canada. Levi Coffin was known as the President of the Underground Railroad.

He married Catharine White, and they settled in New-port (now Fountain City), Indiana. There they lived near a settlement of free African Americans, who aided fugitive slaves. This community needed help, and Levi gave it good management. Two years later Coffin made a trip to North Carolina. He attended a slave auction, during which slaves stood together and were examined by prospective buyers, to determine if they had scars from whip beatings. Even their teeth were examined. He saw a mother, with a one-year-old child in her arms, placed on an auction block. She was rec-ommended by the auctioneer as a good cook and house ser-vant, a hard worker in the fields, and above all, a Christian, as if to claim that God's grace would increase her price. Think-ing that the child would be included in the price, Coffin was sadly mistaken. The child was sold separately. The mother pleaded with her new master to buy the child, but he refused. The child was torn from her mother's arms, and   the mother was dragged away crying, "My child! My child!" Coffin heard the cries of the mother for the remainder of his life.

A Quaker who believed in peace, Levi Coffin was committed to peaceful means to obtain freedom for slaves. He assisted more than one hundred slaves a year to freedom during his twenty years in Newport. He hid fugitive slaves in his home and other homes, barns, cellars, straw sheds, lofts, and attics as places of shelter. He clothed and fed them. As a result, he was often threatened with being hanged, shot, or the burning of his home. Yet he was unrestrained in his devotion to help slaves. Coffin and other anti-slavery workers were ingenious in their methods to assist slaves to freedom. For example, they built wagons, with a secret floor below the upper floor, where slaves could hide. One such wagon has been preserved and is displayed on the Richard Mendenhall property in Jamestown (named for James Mendenhall), North Carolina. Anti-slavery workers created signs to guide fugitive slaves in the direction to travel. Non-perishable food was placed in baskets and hung on trees on the escape routes.

After twenty years in Newport, the Coffins moved to Cincinnati, Ohio, where Levi assisted another one thousand three hundred slaves to freedom. After the Civil War, he campaigned for money to buy food, clothing, and other necessities for freed slaves. He raised more than one hundred thousand dollars for the Freedmen's Aid Association. He journeyed to England, where he was influential in establishing the Englishmen's Freedmen's Aid Society.

Levi Coffin, a friend of the poor and enslaved, was insightful in his work to enlist hundreds of others in the anti-slavery cause. He impacted history in ways that will not be forgotten. He was truly a transformational Quaker leader.

MOSES PEARSON
1798-1874

"My days have been loaded with cares, as my path commonly is as I pass through this world; but I look forward to the end of the race, and my thoughts are, if I can only get the answer of 'Well done,' that will crown all."
-Moses Pearson

Moses Pearson was born into a Quaker family in the Newberry district of South Carolina. He came to Ohio with his parents, and the family settled in Miami County. Moses was raised on a farm, became a carpenter by apprenticeship, and worked as a blacksmith when needed. He built houses and boats, which would carry produce all the way from Ohio to the lower Mississippi River. Moses had a deep religious nature and felt the nearness of God. He endeavored to live by the teachings of Jesus. He read the Bible faithfully and made a *Pocket Memorandum* of Old Testament prophesies of Christ. He often felt an extreme need to pray for others and would pause for prayer at work or in the fields. These prayers sometimes led to action for people in need.

One of Moses Pearson's benevolent actions occurred after Abraham Lincoln was elected President and before he left Springfield, Illinois for Washington. Pearson went to Springfield to talk with Lincoln. When he arrived at Lincoln's office, he found a foyer filled with people waiting to see the recently-elected President. Pearson asked a secretary if he could speak with Lincoln. Pearson was told that he would have to wait his turn. He then asked the secretary to tell Lincoln that he was a Quaker farmer from Ohio, seeking no office, and had a personal message for him. Lincoln immediately sent for Moses, who advised Lincoln not to go through Baltimore on the train to Washington, but to take a different train than had been announced. Later it was made known that the President of the Railroad had become alarmed by rumors of a plot to assassinate Lincoln as he passed through Baltimore. In fact, he had employed detectives to investigate the threat, and they insisted that Lincoln not travel through Baltimore. The only railroad connection then was through Baltimore, but Lincoln took a different train than the one announced.

Now we open another chapter of Moses Pearson's life. He was a loyal member of the Ohio Union Monthly Meeting of Friends and a charter member of the West Branch Quarterly Meeting. When a great need arose he was easily chosen to fulfill it. The Shawnee Native Americans had been forced to move west to an area near Kansas City. The Shawnee Indian Agency sent word to their Quaker friends that they wanted Quakers to come to their new home. Meetings were held in Indiana Yearly Meeting, of which West Branch Quarterly Meeting was a member, and the decision was made that a mission be established among the Shawnees. Moses and his wife, Sarah, and their five children went to the Shawnees and opened the mission. Moses Pearson became the first Superintendent of the Shawnee Mission School. The Pearsons were sensitive to the Native American culture. While they taught Christian values to the students in the school, there was no effort to make them Quakers.

The Pearsons faced challenges. They had unbroken land to prepare for farming and for orchards. Their log house was primitive with only two small rooms. Their annual income was only four hundred dollars to provide for the family. During their time at Shawnee Mission they had two children. Then, after three years of service, having committed to only two years, the Pearsons returned home by steamboats on the Missouri, Mississippi, and Ohio Rivers, which thrilled the children. Following their return they had another daughter.

Sarah Pearson died only four years after returning to Ohio, but Moses lived to be seventy-six. Soon before his death he wrote the words in the quotation at the head of this biographical profile. His desire, that it be said of him, "Well done," was fulfilled.

The Cadburys

John Cadbury
1801-1889

Richard Cadbury
1835-1899

George Cadbury
1839-1922

"The love of family and admiration of friends is much more important than wealth and privilege."
-Richard Cadbury

John Cadbury received his education at Joseph Crosfields Quaker School in Hartshill, England. He was apprenticed in the retail tea trade to John Cudworth, a Quaker. His father gave him funds to work as a tea dealer in Birmingham, England. He set up a shop serving tea, coffee, and chocolate. Eventually, as John's interests in cocoa grew, he opened a factory which produced a variety of chocolate drinks. His brother, Benjamin, joined him in the business, and they named the firm Cadbury Brothers.

John Cadbury became involved in the temperance movement and was an advocate of total abstinence. John wrote in his journal that he traveled through the streets of Birmingham and found five hundred ninety-three licensed liquor sellers and nine hundred seventy-five beer houses in the city. His development of chocolate as a drink was his idea of an alternative to alcoholic beverages.

John was appointed to the Birmingham Board of Street Commissioners and was made overseer and guardian of the poor. He was appalled when he saw young boys working as chimney sweeps. He became a leader in the movement to create machines to clean chimneys. He was troubled by the fact that some of the boys developed twisted backs and damaged joints.

John's concern for the welfare of young people ran parallel to his distress over the ill treatment of animals. As a result, he founded the Animal Friend Society, which was the forerunner of the Royal Society for the Prevention of Cruelty to Animals. John was also appointed to the Steam Engine Committee, which was created to reduce smog in Birmingham. Additionally, he envisioned a model village, which his sons, Richard and George, developed after John's death.

Richard and George, both apprentices in Joseph Rowntree's grocery shop, followed their father's concern for the poor, the less privileged, and troubled people in society and continued reform measures. George developed relationships with employees in the chocolate factory and discussed with them their life problems. He helped them with their education, read aloud to them, shared stories from the Bible, and prayed with them. He worshipped with them each day before work. Richard and George developed "sick clubs" to help with expenses of employees, who needed to take a leave of absence for illness. The brothers were among the first to establish half-workdays on Saturdays and bank holidays. They took employees on leisure outings and played cricket with them. They created an ideal world for their employees.

As the chocolate business grew, the factory was moved to the outskirts of Birmingham in a more rural area, where playing fields and flower gardens surrounded the new work rooms of the factory. Later, houses were built to provide homes for some of the workers, as part of the experiment called Bournville. George and Richard were fulfilling their father's vision for a model village. Bournville became a model for successive generations.

The Cadbury business grew into a great and prosperous enterprise. The health and welfare of the employees remained a high priority for George and Richard, who organized a pension fund and undertook voluntary services. The voluntary services ideal of Bournville was the prototype of voluntary services on a national scale. The Cadbury brothers were also leaders in the emerging Adult School Movement, in which men and women were taught to read, write, and study the Bible. In the Adult Schools students also learned ways to share their faith.

The Cadbury industry flourished. George moved to a larger home as his family grew. He donated his Bournville house to the Society of Friends, and it became known as Woodbrooke, a Quaker study center. Although the Cadbury business grew to great strength financially, and Richard and George became wealthy, they maintained their Quaker values rooted in concern for the less educated and underprivileged. They lived relatively simple lives.

We would prosper by remembering the Cadbury Quakers and their philanthropic work when we eat a Cadbury chocolate bar or a Cadbury chocolate egg.

JOHN GREENLEAF WHITTIER
1807-1892

> *"For all sad words of tongue or pen,*
> *The saddest of these: 'It might have been!'"*
> *-John Greenleaf Whittier*

John Greenleaf Whittier, known as the Quaker poet, was born in a farmhouse near Haverhill, Massachusetts. He aspired to have a political career, but his health declined while he was still young, and his dream vanished. Whittier was greatly influenced by his righteous mother and sister, and by William Lloyd Garrison, who encouraged Whittier to join the anti-slavery movement. He did at age twenty-six. He decided to devote his life to eradicate slavery, war, and intemperance. He aided in the Underground Railroad in New York and Philadelphia and was a delegate to the Philadelphia Anti-slavery Convention. As a consequence of his anti-slavery work, he was mobbed several times at anti-slavery meetings. A Philadelphia mob burned Pennsylvania Hall where he had an office. Whittier disguised himself and managed to rescue his belongings. During the years between 1832 and 1865, Whittier wrote extensively. He authored hundreds of poems, about one third of which addressed the evil of slavery. He also composed numerous religious poems, and in many of them he communicated Quaker beliefs. He penned many prose articles as well.

Whittier was well respected among Friends. The city of Whittier, California was named for him, although he never visited the city. The Quaker college in Whittier, California is named Whittier College. Two Friends churches in the city bear his name, Whittier First Friends Meeting and East Whittier Friends Church. Two streets also are identified by his name, Greenleaf Avenue and Whittier Boulevard.

We are greatly enlightened by Whittier's poetry. In 1834 he wrote a poem entitled, "Hymn," for the meeting of the Anti-Slavery Society at Chatham Street Chapel in New York City. In the poem, which is a prayer, Whittier expressed his anti-slavery sentiment. Here are the closing verses:

And grant, O Father! That the time
Of earth's deliverance may be near,
When every land and tongue and clime
The message of Thy love shall hear;

When smitten as with fire from heaven,
The captive's chain shall sink in dust,
And to his fettered soul be given
The joyous freedom of the just.

Reflecting Whittier's appreciation of the heritage of the Quakers is his poem, "The Quaker of Olden Time." These lines describe clearly Quaker integrity:

The Quaker of olden time!
How calm and firm and true,
Unspotted by its wrong and crime,
He walked the dark earth through.
The lust of power, the love of gain,
The thousand lures of sin
Around him, had no power to stain
The purity within.

The poem, "The Brewing of Soma," better known as "Dear Lord and Father of Mankind," has been sung as a hymn in many Friends Meetings for Worship. The final stanza tells of Elijah's experience on Mount Horeb (I Kings 19:11-12):

Breathe through the heats of our desire
Thy coolness and Thy balm;
Let sense be dumb, let flesh retire;
Speak through the earthquake, wind, and fire,
O still small voice of calm.

Whittier's poem, "The Eternal Goodness," describes his faith in God, who is eternal. Following are two verses everyone should memorize:

I know not what the future hath
Of marvel or surprise,
Assured alone that life and death
His mercy underlies.

I know not where His islands lift,
Their fronded palms in air;

I only know I cannot drift
Beyond His love and care.

John Greenleaf Whittier, an advocate for the poor, the oppressed, and the enslaved was a transformational Quaker
leader. He had an unstoppable commitment to God, whom
he knew as "The Eternal Goodness."

LAURA SMITH HAVILAND
1808-1898

> *". . . After a brief visit with my friends, Levi and Catharine Coffin . . . they were calling me the Superintendent of the Underground Railroad at home."*
> *-Laura Smith Haviland*

Laura Smith was born into a Quaker family in Ontario, Canada. Her father was a minister, and her mother an elder in the Friends Church. At age seven, her family moved to Niagara County in New York, where the closest school was three miles from their home. Laura mainly taught herself through reading books that she borrowed, and she was given assistance from a neighbor. She was greatly influenced by the anti-slavery writings of John Woolman, in which he described the horrible treatment of slaves. Laura, empathetic to African Americans, befriended the few in her town.

At age seventeen Laura married Charles Haviland, and they moved to Raisin Township in Lenawee County, near Adrian, Michigan. Laura and Charles opened the Raisin Institute, a coeducational, integrated school, open to all races where many indigent children were educated. It was the first integrated school in Michigan. Laura and her friend, Elizabeth Chandler, organized the Raisin Anti-Slavery Society. The Havilands made their home a sanctuary for fugitive slaves, and it became a station on the Underground Railroad. Because of their anti-slavery work they were often threatened by gunfire and murder.

A sad ending to a story reveals Laura Haviland's commitment to slaves. A fugitive slave ran to Laura and pleaded for her to rescue his wife, who was still in slavery in Kentucky. Laura made two trips to Kentucky but was unsuccessful in rescuing her. Finally the fugitive slave returned to rescue his wife. They escaped to Indiana, where the pursuers captured them.

Laura traveled through the slave states, sometimes disguising herself, to assist slaves to freedom. On a train near Sylvania, Ohio she was held at gunpoint. Afterward, slave hunters offered a reward of three thousand dollars for her death. The threats only increased her anti-slavery efforts. Further trouble came to Laura when her family contracted the skin disease, erysipelas, from which her mother, father, husband, and one of her children died. She, too, was afflicted with the disease but recovered.

After her husband's death, Laura traveled to other states to aid slaves to freedom. During the Civil War, Laura added to her ministry by giving medical care to wounded soldiers, and improving conditions for war prisoners being held in dehumanizing prisons. When Abraham Lincoln issued the Emancipation Proclamation, many thought the need to aid freed slaves was over, but not Laura Haviland. She was aware that great numbers of them, who were moving to Ohio, Indiana, Illinois, and Kansas were destitute, needing food, clothing, and housing. In response to their critical needs, she volunteered relief services for freed slaves, providing them with food supplies, clothing, housing, seeds for planting, and farm implements. She did extensive relief work in Kansas, where she established schools for freed slaves. The town of Haviland, Kansas, the home of Barclay College, was named for her, as was the former Friends Haviland Academy. She gave the Academy a signed copy of her autobiography, *A Woman's Life Work: Labors and Experiences of Laura S. Haviland*. To this day, her book is read by Barclay College students. A church in the town also bears her name, Haviland Friends Church. Other ministries of Laura Haviland included her leadership in the Great American Revival, advocacy of voting rights for women, and assistance in the organization of the Women's Christian Temperance Union.

Laura Haviland was a humble, yet daring and fearless Quaker leader, who dedicated her life to give freedom to men, women, and children who were oppressed. A statue of Laura Smith Haviland is located in front of the City Hall in Adrian, Michigan.

ELIZABETH COMSTOCK
1815-1891

> *"I rejoice in my gift [of preaching], and it is willingly that I use it."*
> *-Elizabeth Comstock*

Elizabeth Comstock was born into the home of William and Mary Rous, only six miles from the Royal Palace at Windsor in England. She attended Croydon School, after which, she went to Ackworth School. There she was given the position of supervising girls, toward whom she was tender. In 1847, she left Ackworth School and married Leslie Wright. After only two years of marriage, she was grieved by her husband's death. She became a single mother of an infant girl and spent four years in business in Derbyshire. In 1854 she sailed with her daughter and sister to Belleville,

Ontario, where she settled on a farm. During this time, she became involved in a Quaker community and had an awakening to the call of ministry. Soon she was recorded as a Friends minister.

In 1858 Elizabeth married John Comstock and moved to his farm near Adrian, Michigan, the city where a statue of Laura Haviland stands. In this chapter of Elizabeth's life she engaged in the ministry of hospitality in her home, especially to people with problems and difficulties. She also gave service to Quakers and non-Friends in the community.

Elizabeth expanded her ministry and began visiting in other Yearly Meetings. She visited nearly every Yearly Meeting in existence at that time. On her way to Indiana Yearly Meeting she ministered to prisoners at the Indiana State Prison in Michigan City, where she addressed about three hundred prisoners. During her ministry in the Yearly Meetings, Comstock, recognizing the importance of Christian education for Friends, attended Sunday school conventions.

Elizabeth gave leadership in the temperance movement. She befriended Dwight L. Moody, a strong advocate of temperance, and spoke from his pulpit several times. She gave sermons in many Friends Meetings and churches of other denominations and promoted inter-church relationships.

Comstock took up the cause of women's rights, including the right for women to be ministers and preachers. She also became an anti-slavery advocate. She saw slaves beaten, whipped, and treated as property like horses and sheep, considered to be hybrids between beasts and humans. Sickened by the treatment of slaves, Elizabeth made her home a station on the Underground Railroad for fugitive slaves seeking asylum. Living near Canada, she assisted slaves across the border, where they were free and accepted.

Elizabeth Comstock had strong convictions about the Quaker testimony on peace, and was critical of the British government which supported the slave states during the Civil War. She visited in military hospitals in Ohio, Virginia, New York, and Tennessee. She was opposed to the American government's offer for conscientious objectors to pay three hundred dollars as an alternative to participation in the military. That money, she thought, was still another form of support of the war.

Seeing the injustices of slavery, war, and the ill treatment of women, Elizabeth Comstock went into the ghettos of the inner cities, where she ministered to the poor, hungry, and impoverished. With her sensitive and compassionate spirit for the poor and oppressed, and her drive to give them equal opportunity, she would not stop short of talking with the President of the United States about her concerns. She had a conversation with Abraham Lincoln and led worship for him, his wife, Mary Todd Lincoln, and his cabinet.

When the war was over, like Laura Haviland, she realized that freed slaves were in great need of housing, clothing, food, and much more. She raised more than one hundred thousand dollars for freedmen. Later, she approached President Garfield, with whom she had a personal conference for thirty minutes, and appealed for funds for freedmen. As freed slaves were dear to Comstock's heart, so were Native

Americans, many of whom were being mistreated. She went to Wisconsin, where she became a friend to them and ministered to them.

Reflecting on her ministry in America, Elizabeth Comstock estimated that she visited one hundred fifteen thousand prisoners, seventy-four thousand hospital patients, and seventy-four thousand people in institutions for the poor. After her husband's death, she moved to Union Springs, New York, where she spent her final days. Elizabeth Comstock was a true, transformational Quaker leader.

NEREUS PEGG MENDENHALL
1819-1893

> *"[The Bible's] teachings can never fail because they are eternal."*
> *-Nereus Mendenhall*

Nereus Mendenhall was the son of Mary Pegg Mendenhall and Richard Mendenhall, who were North Carolina Quakers. He was the grandson of James Mendenhall. Near the year of his birth the iron plow was invented. The first American Railroad was operating seven years later. Nereus was raised at a time when the rights of Native Americans were being violated, and slavery was the predominant ethical issue. He was blessed to receive his education in a school with Quaker teachers, and which was open to slave children, both boys and girls. Nereus' father was one of the teachers. Nereus had a desire to learn, was mentally alert, and spiritually sensitive. He enjoyed reading, especially the Bible, and doing school lessons. He worked in a printing firm the final four years of high school. Following graduation, he attended Haverford College and graduated with honors.

Nereus returned to North Carolina to serve as Principal of the New Garden Boarding School, but he soon continued his education at Jefferson Medical College. After receiving his degree in medicine, he served as a physician for a few years at his medical clinic in Jamestown, North Carolina but had a growing interest in engineering. This interest led him to civil engineering on railroad construction. For several years, Mendenhall alternated between engineering and teaching at New Garden School. Meanwhile, his love for the Bible kept growing, and he studied the Scriptures in their original languages.

In 1851 he married Oriana Wilson, also a Quaker, and they had five children. During the Civil War they advocated strongly against war and slavery, and provided hiding places for slaves. Nereus, with other Quakers, went to Jefferson Davis, President of the Confederacy, to seek release of imprisoned Quaker conscientious objectors. During the war years, with scarcity of books, paper, food, and oil for lanterns, the New Garden School nearly closed, but Nereus Mendenhall kept it open. Tuition was usually paid in gifts of food.

Mendenhall, knowing that ethical issues were often decided by law, became a state legislator. Moreover, he served as a member of the Board of Directors for the Care of the Mentally Ill and was successful in changing the name of the institution for the mentally ill from asylum to hospital.

Nereus resumed his career as an educator at the Penn Charter School in Philadelphia and at Haverford College. Afterward, he returned to North Carolina and saw the transition from the New Garden School to Guilford College.

Nereus Mendenhall, teacher, school administrator, physician, legislator, engineer, advocate for the enslaved and mentally ill, and a deeply committed Christian was a Quaker leader, who transformed immeasurable numbers of lives.

ALLEN JAY
1831-1910

> *"I believed our Savior meant what He said, when He said 'Thou shalt not kill.'"*
> *-Allen Jay*

Early Years

Allen Jay was a birthright member of the Friends Church. During his early years, he was active in the West Branch Quarterly Meeting in Miami County, Ohio. He and his brother, Eli, built a school building in the unincorporated community of Frederick, where he taught. He also became Principal of the schools in West Milton, near the location where President Hoover's grandparents once lived. Later he moved to Indiana and opened another period of his life, which involved his peace testimony.

Convictions about War

Officials in the American government instituted a draft for conscientious objectors during the Civil War. Jay was opposed to war and refused the draft. A military officer visited Allen Jay and informed him that he was expected to report for training in a military camp at Lafayette, Indiana. Allen told him that his conscience would not allow him to be there, because he could not fight. Since the government permitted conscientious objectors to pay three hundred dollars to hire a substitute, he was offered the option. Allen responded with the quotation at the opening of this profile. After a lengthy conversation the officer left.

Days later he returned and asked Allen to reconsider and to leave an amount of three hundred dollars at a place that he could find the money. Again Jay refused. A third time the officer came and told Allen he was required to sell Jay's property in the amount of three hundred dollars. The officer looked over the farm and selected the livestock to be sold. While he was writing, the Jays prepared dinner. They insisted that he join them for the meal. He accepted. Their conversation at the table made no mention of the officer's work. When they had finished eating, the officer told the Jays that they could make his work less difficult if they would get "mad" at him, or order him out of the house, rather than feeding him and his horse. The Jays told him that they had no ill feelings toward him, since they supposed he was under orders from his superiors.

A few days later when the time arrived for the sale, the officer came to Allen and told him the sale had been postponed. In fact, the sale never occurred. Later Allen discovered that the Governor had approached Abraham Lincoln about the situation, and Lincoln ordered the sale to be stopped. What a remarkable story about the power of Quaker integrity!

Revivalist

Allen Jay was a strong leader in the Great American Revival Movement. He was convincing as a preacher. An illustration of his revival ministry occurred at Highpoint, North Carolina. The pastors of the area came to Allen and asked him to organize a series of revival meetings in the area. He agreed if they would put aside their differences and work in unity. They did work in unity and used the largest church building in the city. It was overflowing with worshippers, and the revival lasted for thirty-one nights.

Commitment to Quaker Colleges

Allen Jay believed strongly in Quaker higher education. He helped Guilford College retire its debt. He contacted members of the House of Representatives, the State Senate, and Andrew Carnegie and was successful in raising substantial funds for Earlham College. To be added to his commitment to Friends higher education was his success in raising a large sum of money for the endowment fund of Whittier College.

International Ministry

Allen sailed to England, where he attended London Yearly Meeting. There he met the Quaker, John Bright, a member of the Parliament. He also ministered among Friends in Norway and Ireland.

The Baltimore Association Experience

Allen became Superintendent of the Baltimore Association. It was formed to give assistance to North Carolina Quakers who were in serious need of food and housing. The Association oversaw the rebuilding of houses, schools, and meetinghouses after the war. Also, instruction was given on operating family farms. One such model farm still exists near Highpoint, North Carolina.

Views on Equality for Women in Ministry

Allen Jay was strongly influenced by George Fox's view of the gospel, which would do away with slavery, oaths, and war, and would give freedom of conscience and equality to women. Therefore, he was a strong advocate for women ministers and women preachers.

This brief profile of Allen Jay only touches on his numerous ministries, but it captures enough of his life to tell us that his Quaker influence was wide and deep, both in America and internationally.

John Walter Malone
1857-1935

Emma Isabel Brown Malone
1860-1924

"Just to think of such a call as that! A call to eternal glory. It is not an invitation for a day, or for a month, or for a year, but for eternity."
-Walter Malone

Walter Malone was the son of John C. and Mary Ann Pennington Malone. Walter's evangelical Quaker roots were nurtured in the rich soil of his boyhood home in New Vienna, Ohio, a vibrant Christian community that was at the time a primary center of Quaker publishing, education, evangelism, and peace work. Walter's faith was shaped in great part by the faithful witness of his mother, who was a recorded Friends minister. It was shaped further by his neighbor, John Henry Douglas, a prominent Quaker evangelist. Walter later moved to Cincinnati where he attended the home church of Levi Coffin, President of the Underground Railroad.

Emma's early faith development was deeply influenced by her Hicksite father, Charles W. Brown, but this liberal theology eventually gave way to a thoroughly orthodox Christian faith. This faith had been consistently modeled by Emma's mother, Margaret Haight Brown, and later reinforced by the ministries of evangelists Esther Frame and D. L. Moody. Walter and Emma were married in 1886, and both learned the way of holiness through Dougan Clark. Together, they became active leaders in the Friends Holiness Movement. They understood it as a call to recover the fervent proclamation of a New Testament gospel that places equal emphasis upon both personal evangelism and social justice.

Walter and Emma became pastors of the Cleveland, Ohio Monthly Meeting of Friends. It was in the midst of that work that they developed a great concern for the young Friends in Cleveland. They saw in them great potential, but they were sorely lacking in adequate training and preparation for church leadership. Furthermore, Walter and Emma were troubled by the liberal schools that were forming. They were determined to have a school with an evangelical Friends theology and solid biblical instruction that would lead to faithful service for Christ and His Kingdom. As Walter put it, "The Spirit therefore impressed it on our hearts to open a small school in which the Bible could be taught every day, and supervision given to prepare students to do practical Christian work, such as visiting the sick, calling in homes, and personal evangelism. Our thought was to teach the Bible in the mornings, and to leave at least a part of the afternoons and evenings free for home mission work."

Chicago Friends invited the Malones to create a Bible school in their city, but they chose a site in Cleveland instead. They rented a vacant house, and in 1892 opened the school with just six students. The first teachers were Walter, who taught New Testament, and Emma, who taught Old Testament. They received no salary, and personally underwrote the school's expenses. Their financial capability came from a stone quarry, which Walter and his brothers owned. Additional financial support was given, and the school expanded. The sole mission of the Cleveland Bible Institute was to train young people for consecrated and dedicated Christian service.

Fifty students eventually enrolled in the first year. Thirteen women from the first class were recorded by Quakers or ordained as ministers by other churches. Two of these women founded a Friends mission in India. Two others were founders of the Church of the Nazarene. By 1900, students from Cleveland Bible Institute had founded or served in five orphanages, twenty shelter homes, and twenty-nine rescue missions. Students did rescue work in a half mile district around Cleveland's Public Square called "the devil's throne." It held 400 saloons, 40 houses of prostitution, and most of Cleveland's gambling resorts, wholesale liquor stores, and opium dens. Each student was assigned a neighborhood in a poor part of town to evangelize and offer social services to the poor. In 1902, two former students, Arthur Chilson and Willis Hotchkiss, in partnership with Edgar Hole, a trustee of the school, founded a new Friends mission field in Kenya. Arthur Chilson and his wife, Edna, were later called to open a new Friends field in Burundi as well. By 1907 the school had missionaries in Brazil, China, Cuba, India, Jamaica, Japan, Kenya, Mexico, South Africa, and Venezuela. The fact that most Friends now live outside the Western world is due, in great part, to Emma's passionate commitment to the

Great Commission, as head of the mission board that took Quakerism to Kenya.

With the need for accreditation, the Bible Institute became a college in 1937 and was re-named Cleveland Bible College, and in 1947 became one of the charter members of the Accrediting Association of Bible Colleges. In 1957 the college moved to Canton, Ohio and became a four-year liberal arts college, with membership in the North Central Association of Colleges. It is now a member of the Higher Learning Commission. The name was changed to Malone College (now Malone University).

Walter and Emma's son-in-law, Byron Osborne, became college president when the school moved to Canton. Everett Cattell, with years of administrative work in India, then succeeded Osborne. Byron and Ruth's daughter, Geraldine Osborne, married John Pennington Williams, who taught at Malone College and later served as academic dean at Friends University. John's parents, Walter and Myrtle Williams, were Friends missionaries to China from 1909-1923. Upon their return to the United States, Walter taught at Cleveland Bible College while pastoring Cleveland First Friends Church. He later served as superintendent of Ohio Yearly Meeting, and authored a number of books, including *The Rich Heritage of Quakerism.* Walter Williams was the grandfather of John P. Williams, Jr., former superintendent of Evangelical Friends Church-Eastern Region, and David O. Williams. David currently serves as director of Evangelical Friends Church International and professor of pastoral ministries at Malone University.

The clear and compelling vision was planted in the hearts of Walter and Emma Malone for raising up Christian workers. Their lives would be fully consecrated to the Lord and to the ministry of the gospel. The Malones are continuing to bear lasting fruit today, not only in North America, but all around the world.

Emma entered the eternal fellowship in 1924 and Walter eleven years later. Shortly before his death, Walter spoke the beautiful words written at the head of this biographical sketch. The Malones were faithful Quaker leaders, who transformed lives with eternal dimensions.

THOMAS RAYMOND KELLY
1893-1941

"There is a Divine Center into which your life can slip, a new and absolute orientation in God, a Center, where you can live with Him, and out of which you can see all of life through new and radiant vision ... It is the life of absolute and complete and holy obedience to the voice of the Shepherd."
-Thomas Kelly

Thomas Kelly was raised in an evangelical Friends home near Londonderry, Ohio. He suffered years of poor health, yet he became active in the Young Friends Movement. During World War I, he served as a volunteer for the American Friends Service Committee in England, where he cared for German prisoners of war. Following the war, Kelly oversaw the food relief program of the Service Committee in Germany.

In his formal education, Kelly attended Wilmington College and Haverford College. He received the Bachelor of Divinity and Doctor of Philosophy degrees at Hartford Theological Seminary. He then taught at Earlham College and later at the University of Hawaii and Haverford College. Kelly served as a visiting professor at Wellesley College, while studying at Harvard University.

A dramatic incident occurred in his life at Harvard. Although Kelly had achieved the degree of Doctor of Philosophy, he wanted a doctorate from Harvard University. He studied diligently and wrote the dissertation. However, during the oral defense of his dissertation, he experienced amnesia, became incoherent, and failed the oral exam. At that time candidates for the Doctor of Philosophy degree were denied a second opportunity. The irreversible failure was devastating to Kelly. He entered into a severe depression, which led to serious thoughts of suicide. President Comfort and Professor Douglas Steere of Haverford College walked the athletic fields with Kelly, reassuring and encouraging him. Months later, the inward battle ceased. Kelly experienced the Holy Spirit illuminating him, and he felt the overwhelming presence of God. His depression had ended.

In his lectures and in his writings, Kelly revealed a deep inward spirit centered in Christ. Two major books are attributed to Kelly: *A Testament of Devotion* and *The Eternal Promise*. *A Testament of Devotion* is included on many lists of historical Christian classics. The chapter titles tell of the spiritual depth of Kelly's thought: "The Light Within," "Holy Obedience," "The Blessed Community," "The Eternal Now and Social Concerns," and "The Simplification of Life." In *The Eternal Promise*, Kelly wrote about the importance of being formed inwardly by Christ, so that there is an enduring awakening of the Divine. These two books were published after Kelly's death from a heart attack at the early age of forty-seven. The message from these books gives clear evidence that Kelly overcame his crushing blow in his failure at Harvard and lived in "holy obedience" to the "voice of the Shepherd."

In our world today, when we experience failures and successes, sorrows and joys, tragedies and triumphs, might we remember the transformational Quaker leader, Thomas Raymond Kelly, and his triumph over his failure.

ERROL T. ELLIOTT
1894-1992

"The hymn, 'I Need Thee Every Hour,' is not enough for me. I need God every minute."
-Errol T. Elliott (near the hour of his wife, Evelyn's, death)

Errol T. Elliott's earliest memories at three-and-a-half years of age were of traveling in a covered wagon drawn by a team of white horses from Missouri to Kansas. He grew up on a farm, where nearby was a one-room school house and a Friends meetinghouse. He remembered being taught by the Quakers about Jesus, the Good Shepherd.

At the age of eight his father died, and the family moved to Haviland, Kansas. He attended Friends Haviland Academy and graduated in 1914. Errol married Ruby Kelly in

1916. Raised as a Quaker pacifist, he became a conscientious objector during World War I and gave voluntary service in France for two years.

Upon his return to the United States, Elliott began preaching and giving pastoral leadership, which he combined with a grocery business. His first pastorate was Rose Valley Friends Meeting, followed by a move to Wichita, where he entered Friends University. He preached on a circuit of four Methodist Churches, until President Mendenhall of Friends University offered him a part-time position as Associate Pastor of University Friends Meeting. Errol graduated from Friends University with a Bachelor's degree. He went on for graduate studies at the Iliff School of Theology and the University of Colorado, while he served the Boulder, Colorado Friends Meeting. He received his Master's degree from the University of Colorado. He also was awarded honorary doctorates from Friends University in 1952 and from Earlham College in 1965.

Following his graduate work, Errol joined the staff of the Five Years Meeting of Friends (now Friends United Meeting) in Richmond, Indiana. In 1936 he accepted the position as Pastor of the Indianapolis First Friends Meeting. It was a sharp contrast to his covered wagon experience on the prairie. During his tenure at First Friends Meeting, World War II had started, and he and E. Raymond Wilson journeyed to Europe to assure Friends there of the love and care of Friends in America.

Having gained significant administrative experience, Errol was called to be President of William Penn College (now

William Penn University) during World War II. The survival of the college was questionable when he assumed leadership because of the financial instability during the war, but Errol managed to keep the college alive. He even sold his family automobile to lessen the pressure on the family budget.

In 1944, Errol returned to the Five Years Meeting of Friends as General Secretary. In this position, he worked for unity among Friends through local and regional conferences. He ministered to Friends worldwide, particularly when he chaired the Friends World Committee for Consultation. He was ecumenical in promoting inter-church relationships. During this period, he was also Editor of *The American Friend* (now *Quaker Life*).

In 1957, Errol accepted a second term as Pastor of the Indianapolis First Friends Meeting, which was his closing pastoral position. Although he was living in Indiana, he continued his international ministry through his visits with Friends around the world and in both the northern and southern hemispheres.

Errol's retirement was his liberation to do extensive research and to write. The results of his research and writing are seen in his classic history book, *Quakers on the American Frontier*. It was followed by *Quaker Profiles from the American West, Life Unfolding: The Spiritual Pilgrimage of a Quaker Plainsman*, his autobiography, and other books. In *Quakers on the American Frontier*, he compared the westward movement of Friends with the history of the early Hebrews. Each moved from an area of slavery through the wilderness of both a physical and spiritual nature. Each maintained a trust that

God would see them through. Both stood on the rim of a new land; however, the Friends used peaceful means, not weapons, to conquer it.

After Ruby's death in 1973, Errol married Evelyn Clark, whom he met at Friends Haviland Academy. They exchanged vows in the traditional manner of Friends. It was done during a Meeting for Worship at University Friends Meeting in Wichita, Kansas, with five hundred worshippers in attendance. Both Errol and Evelyn were active in the ministry of the Meeting. Errol often spoke during the period of open worship, and all ears were open to hear his rich messages.

Errol had a healthy sense of humor. Evidence is his comment from a hospital bed at age eighty-eight. He was awaiting surgery when he told the pastor that he needed to have the operation while he was still young. His personal conversations were colorful and informative from his many years as a Quaker leader. Errol was a very gentle and kind man, with a sensitive spirit toward others who were sick or troubled. He had sound reasoning and a caring heart. All ages of Friends, from the elderly to the children, wanted to be with Errol, because they knew he would have good advice for them.

Errol T. Elliott was born in the nineteenth century and lived in most of the twentieth century. He received his graduate education during the great depression and advocated the Quaker peace testimony through two World Wars. Errol ministered as a pastor, preacher, administrator, college president, general secretary, and teacher. Above all, he was wholly dependent upon God, as his statement above, near the time of Evelyn's death, indicates. He said he needed God "every minute." Errol died in 1992, leaving an enormous legacy for the Religious Society of Friends. We need his life example "every minute."

DAVID ELTON TRUEBLOOD
1900-1994

> *"Quakerism is the most Christ-centered religion. Other religions have liturgies and hierarchies. Quakerism has neither of these. If Quakers do not have Christ, they have nothing."*
> -D. Elton Trueblood

David Elton Trueblood was a prominent, eighth-generation Friend. He was a philosopher, theologian, writer, and church leader. He was born in Pleasantville, Iowa in 1900 and died near Lansdale, Pennsylvania in 1994. He was highly esteemed as the dean of American Religious Writers and published thirty-seven books. Trueblood studied at Brown University, Hartford Theological Seminary, and held degrees from William Penn College (now William Penn University),

Harvard University, and Johns Hopkins University. There he received the Doctor of Philosophy degree. He also held twelve honorary doctorates.

Elton was a devoted husband and father. He married Pauline Goodenow, and following her death, married Virginia Zuttermeister. They would sometimes travel with him when he had speaking engagements. He had four sons and two daughters.

Trueblood served with distinction as Professor at Guilford College, Haverford College, Harvard University, where he was Interim Chaplain, Stanford University, where he was a tenured Professor of Philosophy and Chaplain, Earlham College, and the Earlham School of Religion, which he helped establish as the first Friends seminary. He was also advisor to the Voice of America. Trueblood was Editor of the Quaker periodical, *The Friend*, and was the Clerk of the Friends World Committee for Consultation. Elton was founder and President of the church renewal movement, Yokefellows International, one arm of which was prison ministry. Elton Trueblood was advisor to the American presidents from Hoover to Reagan and served as Chief of the Religious Information Agency under the appointment of President Eisenhower. He was honored to conduct the memorial service for Herbert Hoover. He had friendships with Albert Schweitzer, Reinhold Niebuhr, and Billy Graham, who called him a "true giant of the twentieth century."

Elton Trueblood addressed important topics such as the disciplined life, the ministry of every Christian, and a reasoned, Christ-centered faith. During an interview in his ninetieth year, he identified himself as catholic (meaning non-sectarian); apostolic (being rooted in the New Testament faith); reformed (making changes when needed for improvement); and evangelical (i.e. Christ-centered). About his Christ-centered faith he said that everywhere he went he spoke of the Christlikeness of God. He affirmed Christ as more than a wise teacher. Christ, he said, was his "Savior and Redeemer." Trueblood's major theological work was his book, *A Place to Stand*. In the book he referred to Archimedes, inventor of the lever and pulley, who said that if he had a place to stand he could move the whole earth. But there was another condition. He needed a firm fulcrum. Applying this analogy to his faith, Trueblood affirmed the trustworthiness of Christ as his ultimate act of faith. Christ was his most solid fulcrum and his surest place to stand. Hence he knew Christ personally as his "Center of Certitude." His second chapter in his book, *A Place to Stand*, is "A Center of Certitude."

Elton had a wonderful sense of humor, as was evident when he was invited to be the guest speaker at University Friends Meeting in Wichita, Kansas. The day before he spoke, he told the pastor that he wanted the front pews filled when he delivered his message. The pastor told him that the congregation filled up the back pews and the front ones usually remained empty. Elton countered by saying that Quakers do not bet; nevertheless, he bet the pastor one hundred dollars that the front pews would be full. If he would win, the pastor would give the church a hundred dollars. If the pastor were to win, Elton would do the same. The next morning Elton prefaced his sermon by telling the congregation about the bet. Immediately all the worshippers stood and came forward. Everyone was amused, including the pastor, who reached into his pocket and pulled out one hundred dollars, which he placed in the offering plate.

David Elton Trueblood was a brilliant Quaker transformational leader, teacher, encourager, man of humor, mentor to writers, and advisor to United States Presidents. He made a powerful impact on the Friends movement and the worldwide church in the twentieth century.

ELFRIDA VIPONT FOULDS
1902-1992

"If Quakerism is to remain a dynamic force, it is imperative that, as Friends, we realize that our life is a living sacrament in humility and dedication to God."
-Elfrida Vipont Foulds

Elfrida Vipont Foulds was born in Manchester, England to Quaker parents, Edward Vipont Brown and Dorothy Brown. She attended Manchester High School for Girls and the Mount Quaker Boarding School in York. She continued her education at Manchester University, where she studied history. Following her Manchester educational experience, she studied vocal music in London, Paris, and Leipzig, Germany. She became a professional singer. In 1926 she married R. P. Foulds and gave birth to four daughters. During World War II, Elfrida was head of an evacuation school, where children, including her own, were sent for safety. She became proficient in writing and wrote several children's books, novels, anthologies, biographies, and short stories.

Elfrida Vipont Foulds gave extensive service to the Religious Society of Friends. She served on several committees of London Yearly Meeting, including The Friends Educational Council, The Friends Historical Society Executive Committee, and The Friends Service Council. She was the Clerk of the Meeting for Sufferings Committee, which aided Quakers with urgent needs. She was a member of the committee to oversee Ackworth School, which Dr. John Fothergill was instrumental in establishing. Through her committee work, she served Friends worldwide.

Elfrida's home in later years was in Yealand Conyers. From that small village, Elfrida traveled extensively across England and America. She was a guest speaker at Friends University, a Quaker college in Wichita, Kansas. She spoke with such breathtaking power, that the stories she told are still remembered. Many of her stories included Quakers and their achievements. She conducted pilgrimages to "Quaker Country" in Northwest England, where Quakers had their beginning. She took Friends to places such as, Swarthmoor Hall, which was an early center for Quakers. Pendle Hill, where George Fox had a vision of "a great people to be gathered." Firbank Fell, the location of Fox's preaching for three hours to about one thousand seekers. Lancaster Castle, in which George Fox was imprisoned. Then lastly the Yealand meetinghouse, where Quakers still worship. Elfrida wrote a booklet entitled, *The Birthplace of Quakerism: A Handbook for the 1652 Country*, which is a guide for Quakers touring Northwest England. She generously invited visiting Friends to her home near the Yealand meetinghouse.

On the three-hundredth anniversary of the founding of Quakerism, Elfrida wrote a scholarly history of Quakerism, *The Story of Quakerism through Three Centuries*. She continued as a speaker, author, guide, personal hostess, and was active in the Yealand Meeting through her mature years. She was a faithful Quaker and follower of Jesus Christ. She made her life a "living sacrament given in humility and dedication to God," to which her quotation at the beginning of this biographical profile, calls all Friends. She was a powerful Quaker leader, who transformed lives worldwide. Her tombstone is seen in the Yealand Quaker Meeting burial grounds.

Mildred Turner Neifert
1902-1981

Dan Neifert
1902-2007

> *"Our thoughts were with these people [the Sioux Native Americans]*
> *day and night."*
> *-Mildred Neifert*

Dan Neifert and Mildred Turner Neifert were Quaker leaders. By Christ's guiding presence, they transformed numerous lives through their ministry to children in the public schools, families stricken with poverty, and Native Americans on reservations.

Dan was born near Bloomfield, Nebraska on the family homestead. Mildred was born near Creighton, Nebraska. Both received their Bachelor's degree in 1927, and they were married the same year. Dan's studies continued, and he completed his formal education with a Master's degree from Wichita State University.

Both Mildred and Dan taught in public schools. For thirteen years, they were coordinators of the Southwest Community Center, a self-help ministry to people caught in the web of poverty in Southwest Wichita. During this time, Dan served for a short period as Pastor of the Chapel Friends Church in Wichita.

Dan and Mildred loved and worked closely with Native Americans. They coordinated their work with the Bureau of Indian Affairs, the Associated Committee of Friends on Indian Affairs, the Friends Committee on National Legislation, the Friends World Committee for Consultation, and Civil Service. They ministered among the Sioux Indians on the Sioux Indian reservation at Pine Ridge, South Dakota, where Dan was given the name of "Shield Boy" by Chief Red Cloud's great-grandson. Later they moved to the Hopi Indian reservation in Arizona. Dan taught school, and together with Mildred, built intentional community on the reservation. When their work on the Hopi reservation ended they moved to the Ute Mountain Indian reservation in Colorado. There they developed an adult education program.

Reaching retirement age, Dan and Mildred were not ready to retire. They assumed a ministry among the Osage tribe in Hominy, Oklahoma. Dan was the pastor and preacher at the Hominy Friends Meeting. They wanted to include many others in their work with the Osage Friends, so they conducted work camps, in which volunteers from many churches worked hand-in-hand with the Osage Native Americans. The treats for the volunteers were sharing in Indian meals and participating in Indian dances.

Other virtues, talents, and accomplishments of Dan, during his more than a century of living, are outstanding. He was recorded as a Friends minister. He was an artist, a potter, and a poet. He wrote praise psalms and liturgies. In his later years he often attended worship services with Christians of several different faiths. He was truly ecumenical and was well known by many Christians in Wichita, where they had moved after their Hominy Friends ministry. In his late eighties he learned the German language so that he could read the German family Bible.

Dan and Mildred Neifert lived with the Christian/Quaker values of humility, simplicity, peace, community building, and equality, with love for all people of every race, culture, and ethnicity. They fulfilled Jesus' two greatest commandments, to love God and one's neighbor (Mark 12:29-31).

JACK L. WILLCUTS
1922-1989

> *"The dignity and urgency of Friends ministry comes not from degrees or prestige, but in the humbling knowledge that God has chosen us as recorded in John 15 to be His friends."*
> *-Jack L. Willcuts*

Jack L. Willcuts, a sixth-generation Friend, was born in Burr Oak, Kansas. He graduated from Friends Bible College (now Barclay College) and George Fox College (now George Fox University). At Portland State University he studied journalism. Jack married Geraldine, and they raised three children: Stuart, Susan, and Jannelle.

Jack was a missionary for two terms in Bolivia, a Friends pastor for twenty-six years, and General Superintendent of Northwest Yearly Meeting of Friends for twelve years. He was Editor of the *Northwest Friends* magazine and *Evangelical Friend* magazine. Some of his editorial writings were compiled in the book, *The Sense of the Meeting*. Jack authored *A Family of Friends* and *Why Friends are Friends: Some Quaker Core Convictions*. In the book, *Why Friends are Friends*, Jack wrote on the Friends theology of worship, the sacraments, the ministry of every Christian, peace, the Quaker decision-making process, and being powerful. He co-authored with Myron Goldsmith, *Church Growth in the Soaring Seventies.* He also co-authored *Team Ministry: A Model for Today's Church* with David W. Kingrey, in which he articulated his idea of team ministry. In his pastoral role, Jack effectively developed a team of leaders, who carried out the ministries of the church. In *Team Ministry* he also wrote on the centrality of worship, the necessity of the redemptive fellowship, the imperative of harvest, the need for education, the importance of the family, and the power of being Spirit led.

Jack had the voice of a prophet, the heart of a pastor, the gift of a writer, and the intellect of a teacher. He was warm, gracious, and friendly in his relationships. Jack called Friends to practice their faith in all areas of their living, which Jack, himself, did. He preached about the importance of all Christians discovering God's call for their lives and responding faithfully. He was an encourager to persons of all ages, from the young to the elderly. He saw the God-endowed gifts in others and affirmed them in the development and practice of their talents. The dignity and urgency of his ministry came not from prestige or degrees, but in the humbling knowledge that God had chosen him as recorded in John 15 to be His friend. As God's friend, he had Jesus' blessing of being a transformer for Christ in the world.

Willard Ferguson
1937-2021

Doris Ferguson
1937

"There is no way we can fully express our thankfulness for the way God has led us through all of our lives."
-Doris Ferguson

Willard and Doris Ferguson were Evangelical Friends missionaries in Burundi and Rwanda from 1962 until 2002. Willard's interest in missions began when, as a member of the Friends Bible College (now Barclay College) brass and vocal trio called the King's Kords, traveled to Haiti for a short-term mission trip. There, Willard felt a call to serve as a missionary. From an early age, Doris had intended to be a missionary nurse.

Doris and Willard married in 1959 and moved to Hays, Kansas, where Willard completed a Bachelor's degree and a Master's degree in Biology. Doris received her degree in nursing at Friends Bible College and worked as the college nurse.

They served in Burundi for twenty-three years (1962-1985) where Willard taught. First he was at a teacher training school established by the Friends Church, and later at a Bible school maintained by a consortium of evangelical missions. Doris served as a nurse at the Friends Mission Hospital. They also spent four years as dorm parents at a school for missionary children.

In 1986, the Fergusons were asked to go with George and Dorothy Thomas, long-time Friends missionaries in Burundi, to Rwanda to establish the Friends Church in Rwanda. They would be working under the umbrella of Evangelical Friends Mission. Starting from scratch was very challenging and also very rewarding. Willard's goal was to develop a leadership cohort within the Rwandan community to lead the church. A happy day was turning over the Legal Representative responsibilities to a talented Rwandan pastor.

Willard loved interacting with students and loved teaching. Among his favorite subjects were Creation Science and the Doctrine of Holiness. In Burundi he taught secondary school students, and in Rwanda he taught pastors. Both in Burundi and Rwanda he served as Legal Representative for the mission, and the church.

Burundi and Rwanda are unfortunately well-known for the paroxysms of ethnic violence that have swept these respective countries. Willard and Doris were present in Burundi in 1972, and the tense aftermath of the genocide there, and were evacuated from Rwanda during the Rwandan genocide of 1994. They returned as soon as they could to help rebuild the Friends Church, and aid in the reconciliation efforts in the aftermath of this historic bloodletting. The Fergusons served in Rwanda until September 2002 and spent six months teaching in Burundi in 2004.

The Fergusons returned to the United States, where they became chaplains for a year, ministering to senior residents at Link Care in Fresno, California. They retired to Haviland, Kansas, and both of them became active in Haviland Friends Church. They attended Sunday school and the corporate worship service every Sunday, and served as volunteers in the ministries of the church.

For years they were guest speakers in the Barclay College course on "The Teachings of Friends," in which they shared their experiences on the mission fields in Africa. In their teaching in the Friends classes, Doris told of her experiences of giving water to refugees, when there was a water shortage. She shared that while she gave them water to drink, in order to stay alive, it was about the Living Water offered by Jesus in John 4:10, when he was talking to the Samaritan woman at the well. "If you knew the gift of God, and who it is that is saying to you, 'give me a drink,' you would have asked him, and he would have given you living water." In John 4:14 Jesus explained to the Samaritan woman, "Those who drink of the water that I will give them will never be thirsty." Doris then told the students that Jesus' promise of His living water was also meant for them.

Willard had the opportunity to teach his favorite subjects again, Science and the Doctrine of Holiness, at Barclay College. One of his students wrote this about Willard: "We have all known of his and Doris Ferguson's Christ-filled work amidst the persecution and genocide in Rwanda. But I have the privilege to share how blessed I was to have this godly man as a professor for Doctrine of Holiness . . . The class had its challenges, but this class was far more challenging in personal and spiritual ways. It was the best class I had at Barclay. And who better to teach sanctification than Willard, a pure-hearted man? [I was] very blessed to have known Willard while at Barclay."

Willard entered the eternal fellowship in 2021, leaving an inspiring and enduring model of ministry among Quakers worldwide. Doris has continued her faithful ministries at Barclay College, Haviland Friends Church, the Haviland community, and around the world, as she communicates with her friends in Africa, giving them spiritual encouragement.

PAUL N. ANDERSON
MAY 17, 1956

> *"Apostolic Christianity has less to do with calendars or institutions, and more to do with encountering Jesus Christ personally and being sent by him as a partner in his saving, healing, redeeming work . . . He gives us the keys to a new way of being that not only overcomes the world but also transforms it."*
> *-Paul N. Anderson*

Paul Anderson is Professor of Biblical and Quaker Studies at George Fox University, Extraordinary Professor of Religion at the North-West University of Potchefstroom, South Africa, and Adjunct Professor of New Testament Hermeneutics at Barclay College's School of Graduate Studies. He has also served as a visiting professor or researcher at Yale Divinity School, Princeton Theological Seminary, the University of Mainz, the Radboud University of Nijmegen, and Chapman University. He has a wonderful gift of teaching the Bible so that it lives as a dynamic witness to Jesus Christ.

Paul is the son of Alvin and Lucy Anderson, who taught at Barclay College. Paul's grandfather, Scott T. Clark, was the founding President of Barclay College. He was raised in Colombia, Ecuador, and Dominican Republic. Paul received his Bachelor of Arts degree from Malone University, his Master of Divinity degree from the Earlham School of Religion, and his Doctor of Philosophy degree from Glasgow University.

Paul is internationally renowned for his scholarship in the New Testament, particularly the Johannine literature. He has written numerous books, including *From Crisis to Christ: A Contextual Introduction to the New Testament, The Riddles of the Fourth Gospel,* and *The Christology of the Fourth Gospel.* Paul wrote the commentary on John's Epistles in the *Baker Illustrated Bible Commentary.* His book, *Following Jesus: The Heart of Faith and Practice,* is a masterpiece of rich, practical resources to guide Christians of our generation in a contagious, life-transforming venture of following Jesus.

Paul edited and wrote a new foreword to Elton Trueblood's *A Place to Stand,* and he wrote forewords to five of Henry Cadbury's books, including *George Fox's Book of Miracles.* Paul also wrote forewords to Rudolf Bultmann's *A Commentary on John* and four other books in the Johannine Monograph Series, of which he is a co-editor. He is currently writing the book, *Jesus in Johannine Perspective: A Fourth Quest for Jesus,* and is author or editor of several other published books.

Among other editorial responsibilities, Paul edited *Evangelical Friend* for five years and *Quaker Religious Thought* for eleven years. He is the founding editor of Friends Association for Higher Education's Quakers and the Disciplines Series. He also serves as the New Testament Editor of Brill's Biblical Interpretation Series and served as a co-editor of *Anatomies of the Gospels and Beyond*, a collection in honor of Alan Culpepper. He and Howard Macy edited *Truth's Bright Embrace: Essays and Poems in Honor of Arthur Roberts,* and he co-founded and co-edited five volumes in the John, Jesus, and History Project. His sixth edited volume emerging from that Society of Biblical Literature project is *Archaeology, John, and Jesus: What Recent Discoveries Show Us About Jesus from the Gospel of John*, which is currently in press.

Among the innovations in his work, Anderson was the first New Testament scholar to apply the cognitive-critical works of James Loder and James Fowler to the origins and developments of gospel traditions. It helped showing how eyewitnesses might have come to understand and teach about Jesus and his ministries in somewhat distinctive ways. He was also the first to apply the literary theory of Mikhail Bakhtin to the rhetorical function of gospel narratives, inviting listeners and readers into an imaginary dialogue with Jesus, both then and now. His overall theory of John's dialogical autonomy contributes meaningfully to understandings of John's composition, relations to other traditions, and its emerging historical setting in early Christianity.

In addition to his scholarly work, Paul served in musical and youth ministries and pastored three churches: West River Friends Meeting, Reedwood Friends Church, and Clackamas Park Friends Church. He serves on the Board of Leadership Development of Northwest Yearly Meeting, and he was one of the organizers of the 1985 World Gathering of Young Friends, held at Guildford College in North Carolina.

Supported by the Lilly-funded Congregational Discernment Project grant, Paul was invited to represent Evangelical Friends within the Faith and Order Consultation of the National Council of the Churches of Christ. After Cardinal Kasper invited church leaders to respond to Pope John Paul II's invitation to discern ways forward toward Christian unity, Paul was invited to submit his 16,000-word response to the Vatican, which was also published in *One in Christ* in 2005. Following the lead of Everett Cattell, in his address to Friends in Saint Louis in 1970, Paul articulated a new vision of Christian unity under the Lordship of Jesus Christ. He presented it in person to Pope Benedict and Cardinal Kasper at the Conference of Secretaries of World Christian Communions in Rome the following year. His work on John supported this Spirit-based approach, and he was invited back to the Vatican in 2013. He presented on "The Jesus of History, the Christ of Faith, and the Gospel of John," where he gave Pope Francis a copy of his book, *Following Jesus*.

A leader in the Friends Church, Paul is ecumenical in his vision and outlook. He is a friend to all who know him, and a friend in the spirit of Jesus, who promised, "You are my friends if you do what I command you" (John 15:14). Paul and his wife, Carla, are the loving parents of three grown daughters: Sarah, Della, and Olivia.

Paul N. Anderson, whose life is given to "Following Jesus," has traveled the world over to share the gospel of Jesus

Christ and to advance the most excellent biblical scholarship. He is a true Quaker leader, who continues to transform the world.

The Fraziers of Barclay College

President Emeritus Herbert Hoover Frazier
March 4, 1929

Shirley (Nuffer) Frazier
May 5, 1932

President Royce Eldon Frazier
August 15, 1952

Carolyn Louise (Binford) Frazier
December 20, 1952

"Transformational leaders work to place people in their sweet spot so they, and the organization, can soar!"
-Royce Frazier

Herbert Hoover Frazier

Herbert (Herb) Hoover Frazier was named for the President of the United States, because he was born on the day that Herbert Hoover was inaugurated as President, March 4, 1929. He was born in Santa Barbara, California. His parents were Ivan and Julia (Palmer) Frazier. Herb's family moved to

Kansas when he was two years old, and his father pastored various churches in Mid-America Yearly Meeting. He graduated from Friends Haviland Academy, received the Bachelor's degree from Emporia State University, and the Master's degree in School Administration from the University of Kansas. Additionally, he was granted the National Science Foundation Scholarship to the University of Alabama. Herb was awarded the honorary degree, Doctor of Theological Education, which was bestowed upon him by Barclay College. When he turned over the presidency to Royce Frazier, his son, he was honored further with the title, President Emeritus.

Herb spent two years in the United States Army, after which he taught in schools in Lyon County, Wisley, Overland Park, Wichita, Hugoton, Greensburg, and Haviland, Kansas. Following his public school teaching, he assumed the role of Academic Dean for eight years and Director of Admissions for six years at Friends Bible College (now Barclay College). With his academic background, he also supervised teachers in training. Having administrative experience, he was called by Mid-America Yearly Meeting to be Administrative Assistant. Subsequently, Herb returned to Barclay College to work first in the development department and then to serve as President of the college.

Herb gave leadership in Friends Churches, in which he taught Junior-age youth and was Superintendent of Junior Sunday School Departments in Wichita Friends Chapel Church and Haviland Friends Church. He and Shirley sponsored high school and college youth groups, and they directed the Mid-America Yearly Meeting Junior High Quiz Program for ten years.

Shirley (Nuffer) Frazier

Shirley (Nuffer) Frazier was born May 5, 1932 in Emporia, Kansas to parents Oscar and Sophia (Gurtler) Nuffer. She grew up in the Emporia Friends Church, graduated from Emporia High School, and attended Emporia State University. She and Herb married and have worked as a team all of their married life. Shirley has been active in the church her entire life. She had a ministry of secretarial work for thirty-one years: three years at Friends Bible College, twenty-three years at Haviland Friends Church, and five years at the Mid-America Yearly Meeting office. A talented musician, she was pianist for a church in San Antonio, Texas, Emporia Friends Church, Wichita Friends Chapel Church, and Haviland Friends Church. She also taught Sunday school for junior-age girls. Shirley continues her volunteer ministry at Barclay College, making phone calls to campus personnel and arranging for refreshments for campus events. Meanwhile, Herb, age 93, now Archivist of the college, works at his desk every day.

Herb and Shirley have three lovely children: Royce, Kevin, and Lori, ten grandchildren, and twenty-three great-grandchildren.

Royce Eldon Frazier

Royce Eldon Frazier was born on August 15, 1952 to Herbert Frazier and Shirley (Nuffer) Frazier in San Antonio, Texas, where his father was stationed after being drafted into the Army. Soon the family moved to Kansas City, and there his father took a teaching position. The family moved to Wichita, Kansas in 1960, where his father taught at Brooks Junior High School. While in Wichita, Royce developed a love for sports and music. Living in a neighborhood with many neighbor children, the Frazier backyard became the stadium for whiffle ball games in the summer and football in the winter.

In the seventh grade Royce became a paper boy for the "Wichita Eagle and Beacon." He bought his first new bike with his earnings and paid his parents back $5.00 a month until the $60.00 Spider bicycle was his. It was a silver beauty.

Royce recalls that a speaker at camp called campers to commit their lives fully to Christ. In that moment he realized that all he could give to Jesus could not fully repay what Jesus had fully given to him through His love and His sacrifice. That moment was a point when he fully surrendered to Christ. That moment changed his life completely.

At the end of Royce's ninth grade year the family moved to Haviland, Kansas, where Herb became the Academic Dean at Friends Bible College and Friends Haviland Academy. It was a difficult move until a young farm girl caught his eye. Royce and Carolyn (Binford) dated through high school and married after their sophomore year of college on May 13, 1972 at Haviland Friends Church. Royce completed his Bachelor's degree in Bible from Friends Bible College, and both Royce and Carolyn finished their teaching degrees at Emporia State University in 1975. Royce continued his education, achieving the Master of Science degree in Marriage and Family Therapy (clinical) at Friends University, the Master of Arts degree in Psychology (clinical) at Fielding Graduate University in Santa Barbara, California, and the Doctor of Philosophy degree in Psychology (clinical) at Fielding Graduate University.

Royce had a rich and varied career path. He taught and coached at Greensburg High School and Oklahoma Bible Academy, which provided fulfillment for his great love of sports. Then God surprised him by calling him to serve as Superintendent of Youth Ministries for Mid-America Yearly Meeting of Friends for eighteen years. He entered private clinical practice for a number of years to work more directly with broken and hurting individuals and families. Finally, he accepted the position of Vice President for Academic Services at Barclay College to develop the online degree program, and he eventually became President.

Royce's greatest love is his wife, Carolyn, and his family. He prides himself on being an "elf," and always making Christmas a special family time of celebration. He loves cold weather, a warm fire, Christmas, Thanksgiving, popcorn, hot coffee, and making breakfast for the family. He distinguished himself as the city boy, who took a neighboring farmer's new combine and cut the weeds in the ditch in front of his house. He worked for a while at the Binford Brothers Dairy Farm.

His greatest professional passion has been to make people around him better and to help them find their sweet spot. His goal in life has been to give himself to something that would outlive him-- his kids and grandkids, Barclay College, and his faith. Royce's life verse is Micah (6:8 NIV). "And what does the Lord require of you? To act justly and to love mercy and to walk humbly with your God."

Royce and Carolyn are the loving parents of three talented children: Lance, Jeremie, and Shelby. They have twelve beautiful grandchildren.

Carolyn Louise (Binford) Frazier

Carolyn Louise (Binford) Frazier was born on December 20, 1952 to Allen Binford and Mary (McNichols) Binford in Pratt, Kansas. Allen farmed on the family farm east of Haviland, Kansas. The family residence was in Wellsford, Kansas. Mary worked in the kitchen at the Friends Haviland Academy. Both sets of grandparents lived in Haviland.

Carolyn grew up on the farm and was the second oldest of five children. Her two sisters had allergies that limited their work on the farm, so Carolyn spent much of her growing up years working with her dad, driving tractors and trucks and working as a hired hand. The family also operated Binford Brothers Dairy with her uncle Paul Binford until 1972. These years cultivated a great love for the outdoors, which she carries to this day.

Carolyn attended Wellsford Grade School until the fifth grade. There were a total of eleven students and two teachers in the school. In the fifth grade the school closed, and all the students went to Haviland Grade School.

Carolyn recalls her first experience in accepting Jesus was when her older sister took her to the altar with her at a camp meeting in Haviland when she was in the first grade.

However, her personal choice to follow Jesus came when she went forward during a Sunday morning service at the Haviland Friends Church when she was in the third grade. That began a lifetime of faithful commitment to the call of Christ.

Carolyn was always active in music and sports. She was a cheerleader in grade school, high school, and college. She was voted "Best All-Around" by her peers as a freshman at Friends Haviland Academy, and she and Royce were homecoming king and queen at Barclay College. She sang in a trio through high school called the Golden Tones with her best friends, Cindy Robinson and Roberta Barnett, and traveled throughout the mid-west ministering in churches. In college she was in choir and traveled for two years in a small music ensemble throughout the United States presenting in churches and high schools. Since the 1990's she has served an active role in music at Haviland Friends Church.

When she was a sophomore in high school a young man named Royce Frazier moved to town. They started dating the spring of their sophomore year in high school. Royce and Carolyn dated through high school and married after their sophomore year of college on May 13, 1972 at Haviland Friends Church. Carolyn completed her Bachelor of Education degree in Family and Consumer Science at Emporia State University in 1975.

In her career as a teacher, Carolyn taught at Haviland High School. During a seven-year period she also taught at Greensburg High School concurrently with her duties at Haviland High School. When Haviland High School closed she moved to the grade school in Haviland and taught kindergarten until her retirement. In 2021 she came out of retirement to teach a Life Skills class in the Haviland Junior High program where she is privileged to teach two of her grandchildren, Jace and Hallie. Carolyn also carries responsibilities in the Barclay College registrar's office. In whatever setting Carolyn lives and works, her very presence radiates brilliantly the light, peace, tenderness, and love of Christ.

Carolyn's greatest love is her family. She loves the outdoors, water skiing, snow skiing, and making things grow. She can still slalom water ski. Royce calls their home in the country 'Carolyn State Park' because of all the flowers. She collects her own seeds and bulbs and starts flowers from seeds in her greenhouse in the winter. She is a quilter and since 1990 has donated one or two quilts each year to the Barclay College Ladies Auxiliary Sale. She also is responsible for the landscaping at Barclay College, giving it a splash of color during the spring, summer, and fall.

Carolyn loves her grandkids and having them home. She enjoys teaching them to cook, bake, make crafts, sew, work in the yard, and discover the skills and creativity within themselves. She loves summer, planting, making the yard look great, and zooming around on her mower. She is in her happy place when the kids come home and the house is buzzing with noise and laughter.

Additional Frazier Ministries at Barclay College and Worldwide

Herb and Shirley (with friends whom they encouraged to donate) saved Barclay College, following a proposal to close the college, which had been made before Herb became President. Herb and Shirley had a vision of a prosperous future for the college. They were determined to keep the doors of the college open and, under Herb's presidency and Shirley's strong encouragement, they did. Their vision has been fulfilled beyond what they imagined.

Royce and Carolyn, Christ-centered leaders, know that "Transformational leaders work to place people in their sweet spot so they, and the organization, can soar." Indeed, Royce has placed the members of the Barclay College family in their sweet spot, and they and the college, are soaring. By the grace of God, Barclay College, under Royce's Presidency and with the multi-faceted responsibilities of Carolyn, is prospering greatly. The college now has full accreditation in the Higher Learning Commission. Enrollment has increased with full tuition scholarships for undergraduate students. Barclay College has enrolled students from many nations in six continents around the world to study and earn degrees. The Craziers, with the support of the college community, raised millions of dollars for the Ross/Ellis Fine Arts Center. They have added Bachelor's degree programs in Criminal Justice and Nursing, and a School of Graduate Studies, offering a Master of Arts degree in Theology with several concentrations. Moreover, the development of a Wellness Center is now underway. Throughout these additions and enhancements, Royce and Carolyn have directed a financial campaign, resulting in a substantial increase in the college endowment. Additionally, Carolyn and Royce have a lovely ministry of hospitality, in which they regularly invite all the college faculty, administrators, staff, and board of trustee members to their home for fellowship and refreshments. They make the college a warm, caring, and beautiful family.

Herb, Shirley, Royce, and Carolyn Frazier claim no success from themselves. They know that the success comes from the abundant blessings of an all-gracious God. They have a deep Quaker faith. They are active members in Haviland Friends Church, where Royce and Carolyn play instruments in the church orchestra and they are steadfast in prayer. They pray daily for members of the college community.

The Fraziers have brought Barclay College to exceptional heights of spiritual and academic life, as they have committed themselves to prepare students in a Bible-centered environment for effective Christian life, service, and leadership that will be transforming. Herb, Shirley, Royce, and Carolyn Frazier are true, visionary, Quaker leaders, who are transforming the world.

BIBLIOGRAPHY

Anderson, Paul. *Elizabeth Fry – A Noteworthy Friend*. Northwest Yearly Meeting *Connection*, March 29, 2019.

Angell, Stephen. W. *Christian History*. Issue 117.

Barbour, Hugh, and Arthur O. Roberts, eds. *Early Quaker Writings*. Grand Rapids, Michigan: William B. Eerdman's Publishing Company, 1973.

Barbour, Hugh, and J. William Frost. *The Quakers*. Richmond, Indiana: Friends United Press, 1994.

Barclay, Robert. *Barclay's Apology in Modern English*, Edited by Dean Freiday. Newberg: Barclay Press, 1991.

Braithwaite, William C. *The Beginnings of Quakerism*. York, England: William Sessions Limited, 1970.

Cadbury, Deborah. *Chocolate Wars: The Rivalry between the World's Greatest Chocolate Makers*. New York: Public Affairs, 2010.

Christian Faith and Practice in the Experience of the Society of Friends. London: London Yearly Meeting of the Religious Society of Friends, 1960.

Elliott, Errol T. *Life Unfolding: The Spiritual Pilgrimage of a Quaker Plainsman*. Richmond, Indiana: Friends United Press, 1975.

Elliott, Errol T. *Quaker Profiles from the American West*. Richmond, Indiana: Friends United Press, 1972.

Elliott, Errol T. *Quakers on the American Frontier.* Richmond, Indiana: Friends United Press, 1969.

Essays written by Hannah and Jasmine Williams, great-great-granddaughters of Walter and Emma Malone, in a Barclay College course on "The Teachings of Friends."

Foster, Richard J., and Kathryn A. Helmers. *Life with God: Reading the Bible for Spiritual Transformation.* New York: Harper One, 2010.

Foulds, Elfrida Vipont. *The Birthplace of Quakerism: A Handbook for the 1652 Country.* London: Quaker Books, 1960.

Fox, George. *The Journal of George Fox,* Edited by John L. Nickalls. Philadelphia: Philadelphia Yearly Meeting of the Religious Society of Friends, 2005.

Gurney, Joseph John. *A Letter to a Friend on the Authority, Purpose, and Effects of Christianity, and Especially on the Doctrine of Redemption.* London, 1835 in Thomas D. Hamm, ed. *Quaker Writings: An Anthology, 1650-1920.* New York: Penguin Books, 2010.

Hamm, Thomas D., ed. *Quaker Writings: An Anthology, 1650-1920.* New York: Penguin Books, 2010.

Haviland, Laura Smith. *A Woman's Life Work: Labors and Experiences of Laura S. Haviland.* Cincinnati: Walden and Stowe, 1882.

Hinshaw, Seth B. *The Carolina Quaker Experience 1665-1958.* North Carolina Yearly Meeting, 1984.

Hodgkin, L. V. *A Book of Quaker Saints.* London: Friends Home Service Committee, 1972.

Jackson, Sheldon. *A Short History of Kansas Yearly Meeting.* Day's Print Shop, 1946.

Jay, Allen. *Autobiography of Allen Jay 1831-1910.* Richmond, Indiana: Friends United Press, 2010.

Jones, Rufus M. *The Later Periods of Quakerism Volume I.* Westport, Connecticut: Greenwood Press, 1970.

Jones, Rufus M. *The Later Periods of Quakerism Volume II.* Westport, Connecticut: Greenwood Press, 1970.

Jones, Rufus M. *Quakers in the American Colonies.* New York: Russell and Russell, Inc., 1962.

Kelly, Thomas. *A Testament of Devotion.* New York: Harper and Brothers Publishers, 1941.

Kelly, Thomas. *The Eternal Promise.* Richmond, Indiana: Friends United Press, 1977.

Leppert, Glenn. *The Heart of Friends; Quaker History and Beliefs.* Haviland, Kansas: Barclay College Publishers, 2020.

Neifert, Mildred. *My Rememberings, 1976.*

Newby, James. *Elton Trueblood: Believer, Teacher, and Friend.* San Francisco: Harper and Row, Publishers, 1990.

Oliver, John W., ed. *J. Walter Malone: The Autobiography of an Evangelical Quaker.* Lanham, MD: University Press, 1993.

Oliver, John W. *A Quaker Vision for Education.* Canton, OH: Oliver House Publishing, 2013.

Osborne, Byron L. *The Malone Story: The Dream of Two Quaker Young People.* Newton, KS: United Printing, 1970.

Penn, William. *Fruits of Solitude*. Richmond, Indiana: Friends United Press, 1978.

Penn, William. *No Cross, No Crown*. Richmond, Indiana: Friends United Press, 1982.

Punshon, John. *Portrait in Grey: A Short History of the Quakers*. London: Quaker Books, 2006.

Quaker Faith and Practice, The Book of Christian Discipline of the Yearly Meeting of the Religious Society of Friends (Quakers) in Great Britain, 1995.

Russell, Elbert. *The History of Quakerism*. Richmond, Indiana: Friends United Press, 1979.

Thomas, C. Yvonne Bell. *Roads to Jamestown*. Fredericksburg, Virginia: Bookcrafters, 1997.

Trueblood, Elton. *A Place to Stand*. New York: Harper and Row, Publishers, 1969.

Trueblood, D. Elton. *I Wish I had Known Joseph John Gurney*. *Quaker Life* Magazine, July-August, 1984.

Trueblood, D. Elton. *Robert Barclay*. New York: Harper and Row, Publishers, 1968.

Trueblood, D. Elton. *The People Called Quakers*. New York: Harper and Row, Publishers, 1966.

Trueblood, Elton. *While It Is Day: An Autobiography*. New York: Harper and Row, Publishers, 1974.

Vipont, Elfrida. *A Faith to Live By*. Philadelphia: The Religious Education Committee of the Friends General Conference, 1962.

Vipont, Elfrida. *The Story of Quakerism through Three Centuries*. London: The Bannisdale Press, 1960.

Whittier, John Greenleaf. *The Complete Poetical Works of John Greenleaf Whittier*. Boston: Houghton, Mifflin and Company, 1984.

Williams, Walter. *The Rich Heritage of Quakerism*. Newberg: Barclay Press, 1987.

Woolman, John. *The Journal of John Woolman*. Secaucus, New Jersey: The Citadel Press, 1961.

https://www.quakersintheworld.org/quakers-in-action/14/Margaret-Fell.

https://www.quakersintheworld.org/quakers-in-action/223/Elizabeth-Hooton.

https://www.quakersintheworld.org/quakers-in-action/270/George-Cadbury.

https://www.quakersintheworld.org/quakers-in-action/16/John-Cadbury.

https://www.quakersintheworld.org/quakers-in-action/269/Richard-Cadbury.

http://www.collectingbooksandmagazines.com/vipont.html.

Acknowledgments

I am grateful to Royce Frazier for encouraging me to write this book, Derek Brown for writing the foreword and his oversight of the publication, Trent Maggard for his technical assistance, David Williams for his contributions to the profile of Walter and Emma Malone, Dean Ferguson for his contributions to the profile of Willard and Doris Ferguson, Randy and Carol Mullikin for their contributions to the profile of Dan and Mildred Neifert, and Rachel Mortimer for advancing the manuscript to a completed book form.

ABOUT THE AUTHOR

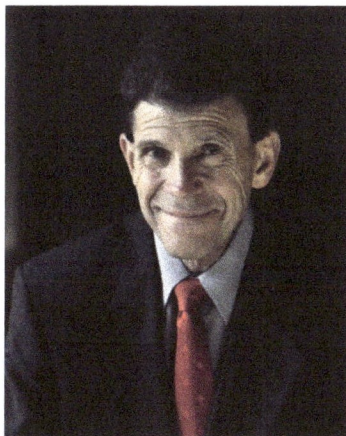

David Kingrey has been a Friend his entire life. He received the degrees of Bachelor of Arts in Religion, Master of Ministry, and Doctor of Ministry. A Recorded Minister in the Friends Church, David has served in leadership in Friends Churches for more than fifty years. At Barclay College, David has chaired the Bible/Theology Department. He has also served as Director and Professor of the Quaker Studies and Spiritual Formation concentrations in the School of Graduate Studies. David is currently Chair of the Biblical Studies Online Program. He has ministered and built friendships with the larger family of Friends in six continents and has co-authored three books: *Now Is Tomorrow, Team Ministry,* and *The Heart of Friends; Quaker History and Beliefs.* His favorite pastime is relaxing with his family. David is married to Carol, and they have two sons, David and Scott.

www.ingramcontent.com/pod-product-compliance
Lightning Source LLC
Chambersburg PA
CBHW070638150426
42811CB00050B/383